CW01072666

EXPERT SYSTEM DEVELOPMENT IN PROLOG AND TURBO-PROLOG™

PETER SMITH

SIGMA PRESS
Wilmslow, Cheshire, U.K.

HALSTED PRESS
a division of JOHN WILEY & SONS, Inc.
605 Third Avenue, New York, N.Y. 10158
New York • Chichester • Brisbane • Toronto • Singapore

Copyright © P Smith, 1988.

Reprinted 1988

All Rights Reserved. No part of this publication may be reproduced, stored in a retrieval system, or transmitted in any form or by any means, electronic, mechanical, photocopying, recording or otherwise, without prior written permission.

First published in 1988 by
Sigma Press 98a Water Lane, Wilmslow, SK9 5BB, England.

British Library Cataloguing in Publication Data
Smith, P. R. (Peter)
     Expert system development in Prolog and Turbo-Prolog.
     1. Artificial intelligence - Data
     processing 2. Prolog (Computer program
     language)
     I. Title
     006.3'028'55133   Q336

Library of Congress Cataloguing in Publication Data
Smith, P. R. (Peter R.)
     Expert system development in Prolog and Turbo-Prolog.
     Bibliography: p.
     Includes index.
     1. Expert systems (Computer science) 2. Prolog
     (Computer program language) 3. Turbo Prolog (Computer
     program) I. Title.
     QA76.76.E95S65 1987 006.3'3 87-14690

ISBN (Sigma Press): 1-85058-064-2

ISBN (Halsted Press):   0-470-20911-9

Distributed by
John Wiley & Sons Ltd., Baffins Lane, Chichester, West Sussex, England.

Halsted Press, a division of John Wiley & Sons Inc, 605 Third Avenue, New York, NY 10158, USA

Printed by J. W. Arrowsmith Ltd., Bristol

Cover design based on *The Decameron* by John W Waterhouse (1849 - 1917); the original painting hangs in the Lady Lever Art Gallery, Port Sunlight, England and is reproduced with their permission.

Acknowledgments:
IBM,PC are trademarks of International Business Machines
DEC, VAX are trademarks of Digital Equipment Corporation
Turbo Prolog is a trademark of Borland International Inc.

PREFACE

The area of expert systems has previously been largely the territory of the academic and the researcher with few practical applications in commerce or industry. It appears now, however, that industry is beginning to wake up to the potential of such systems to produce cost effective solutions to their problems. It is towards the concept of the practical use of expert systems that this book is aimed.

The book is designed for the reader who requires a practical treatment of the applications of the Prolog programming language and its relevance in expert system design and implementation. It is envisaged that the book will thus be useful to students on a degree course which contains an artificial intelligence component, computer professionals who are about to enter, or are interested in, the expert systems field and computer hobbyists who wish to become involved in this new and exciting area. The book assumes no previous programming knowledge, although an understanding of very basic computing terminology is expected.

The book begins by discussing the concept of expert systems and explaining the components of an expert system. Recent initiatives in the area (Alvey, the Japanese Fifth Generation Project) are also discussed. The reader is then taken through the concept of knowledge engineering before being introduced to the role of Prolog in expert system design.

The following six chapters are devoted to coverage of the Prolog language with the emphasis on its application in expert systems. The objective of these chapters is to enable the reader to come to grips with Prolog so that he will be able to develop his own expert systems. Although it is true that Prolog is now quite widely available of many microcomputers, the language itself is less well known than languages such as BASIC and Pascal; it was for this reason that such detailed coverage of its structure and operation has been included.

These chapters, then, guide the reader through the structures of the Prolog language. Each chapter contains sample Prolog programs which act as an illustration of such important features as pattern matching, recursion, list manipulation, backtracking and the cut. The extensive debugging facilities available within the Prolog environment are introduced at an early stage to enable the reader to apply these during the development of his software. Each chapter also contains a selection of Prolog programs and relevant exercises which may be used for class work or as a self study text. Solutions to selected exercises are presented at the end of the text.

Chapter 9 of the book is devoted to coverage of the problems of user-interface design and explains how Prolog can be used to develop expert systems with extremely friendly and "intelligent" interfaces.

Chapter 10 is devoted to a detailed coverage of the development of one particular expert system, designed to classify pedigree dogs. The reader is taken through each stage of the design of the basic expert system, before being shown how it can be extended to a system which can itself learn new "knowledge" and explain its conclusions.

The final chapter of the text contains a series of case studies. Each case study comprises full coverage of the implementation (in Prolog) and operation of a "mini" expert system. The case studies are chosen from several different subject areas but are designed to be comprehensible to the general reader who has no specialised knowledge of that area. One of these case studies is in Turbo Prolog to provide an illustration of that particular dialect of the language.

The book is based on the "Edinburgh syntax" version of Prolog and all of the programs in the text have been developed and tested on a DEC VAX 11/750 computer, using the POPLOG environment (which was developed at Sussex University and is marketed by Systems Designers International).

Each chapter containing coverage of the syntax of Prolog also includes a "Notes for Turbo Prolog programmers" section, which aims to highlight the differences between the Edinburgh syntax version of the language and Turbo Prolog. These sections provide brief notes which will prove useful to those readers who are intending to program in Turbo Prolog.

ACKNOWLEDGEMENTS

This book has developed as a result of teaching Prolog to Final Year undergraduates on the Computer Studies option within the B.Sc Combined Studies in Science course at Sunderland Polytechnic and, as such, is the result of many discussions with the students who have passed through that course over the last few years. I am grateful to those students, too numerous to mention, who have provided me with a large number of useful examples and opinions relating to Prolog.

I would also like to thank my colleagues at Sunderland for their support and encouragement throughout the life of this project, in particular Tom Ormerod for his help and advice on the teaching of Prolog, David Murton for his technical assistance and advice on the use of the word processor, and Marc Roper for allowing me to use part of his Ph.D project for one of the case studies in Chapter 10. I would also like to express my gratitude to my family for the patience and encouragement which they have shown me throughout the writing of this book and to my parents for proof reading several versions of the manuscript.

CONTENTS

Chapter 1

EXPERT SYSTEMS

1.1 What is an expert system?

The earliest computers were extremely large awe-inspiring machines which were used by scientists to perform rapid calculations. In order to obtain an answer from these strange looking beasts the user would first have to decide on a method of solving his problem. He would then have to translate his method of solution into a set of instructions called a computer program. The program would invariably have to be written in a language that was unintelligible to the average human being and would consist of a series of strange commands which related to the way in which the computer's electronic components operated.

Since those early days computer designers have striven to make computers easier to use; to bridge the gap between man and machine. The languages in which the user has to write his computer program have been designed so that they resemble, as closely as possible, the English words and phrases and mathematical symbols which we use in everyday life. The computer hardware itself has seen dramatic reductions both in price and size, accompanied by similarly dramatic increases in its capacity to store and process data.

But still the computer is only a machine. We cannot (yet) talk to it in English as we would a human being. We cannot give it an everyday problem to solve unless it has already been programmed with an appropriate method of solution. We cannot expect it to learn from its mistakes and apply previous experience and common sense to the solution of problems. Or can we?

Artificial Intelligence (AI) is the name given to a field of research which is attempting, with varying degrees of success, to produce computer systems which can accomplish the above. In other words, the aim of AI research is to provide computers with similar intellectual abilities to those of a human being. This is obviously an awesome task, particularly as many of our own intellectual abilities and mental processes are not yet fully understood, even by experts in psychology.

One area of AI research which is quite advanced, however, is that of expert systems. Indeed, expert systems is one of the few areas of AI which has moved out of the research laboratory and into the real world and is beginning to realise its potential in industrial and commercial applications.

An expert system is a computer system which can act as a human expert within one particular field of knowledge. That is, an expert system embodies knowledge about one specific problem domain, and possesses the ability to apply this knowledge to solve problems from that problem domain. Ideally the expert system can also learn from its mistakes, and gain experience from its successes and failures. The system should also be able to explain the reasoning behind the way in which it has arrived at a particular conclusion.

You may ask "Why do we need a computer to do this task for us? We have plenty of human experts to solve our problems for us".

But is that true?

Consider the following properties of human experts:

> They are scarce.
> Their services are expensive.
> They are usually very much in demand and are very busy.
> They are mortal.

Expert systems do not suffer from the above drawbacks.
Consider the following scenario:

Red Adair is an expert at extinguishing oilwell fires. He is also extremely expensive to hire and it is likely that on his demise all of his vast expertise will be lost. Wouldn't it be useful, and indeed sensible, if all that expertise could somehow be implanted within a computer system? A copy of this system could then be established at every major oilwell in the world and, in the event of an emergency, the system could be used as an extremely cost-effective consultant.

There are many other fields of enterprise where such a system would be of immense value. Section 1.3 of this chapter discusses some of the applications of expert systems technology in more detail.

1.2 The components of an expert system

An expert system comprises three basic components as illustrated in Figure 1.1. These components are:

> a knowledge base
> an inference engine
> a user interface

We will now explain each of these three components in more detail.

The knowledge base comprises a series of facts and rules about the particular problem area from which the system draws its expertise (often termed the problem domain). For instance, an expert system which is designed to aid medical practitioners in the diagnosis of abdominal pain would have a knowledge base which contained facts and rules about the likely causes of such pain, and the particular symptoms related to each of these causes.

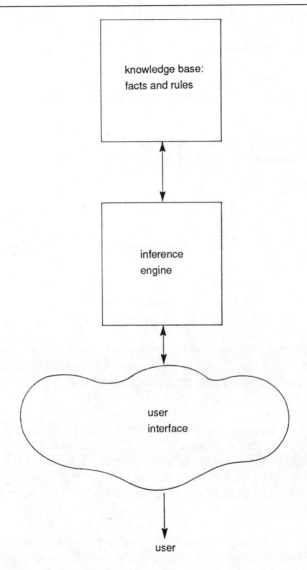

Fig 1.1 Components of an expert system

A fact is a clear, concise statement which expresses something which is true within the particular problem domain. For example, the following statements are all facts:

John is a man.
John lives in a house.
Tony drives a car.
Mary has brown hair.

A rule is generally of the form

if statement1 then statement2

where statement1 and statement2 are both expressions which may or may not be true. The rule is simply stating that if statement1 is true then this implies that statement2 is also true. Examples of rules are:

If a man marries twice, then he is a bigamist.
If a person has $1,000,000, then he is a millionaire.

Consider an expert system which is designed to enable the classification of animals. The knowledge base of such a system might contain the following facts and rules:

Facts: A mammal is an animal.
A bird is an animal.

Rules: If an animal gives milk then the animal is a mammal.
If an animal has feathers then the animal is a bird.
If an animal builds a nest and lays eggs then the animal is a bird.

Such facts and rules must be expressed in terms of an appropriate programming language such as Prolog. By the time you have worked through this book you will be fully competent in Prolog and able to devise and implement your own knowledge bases.

In order to make use of the expertise which is embodied in the knowledge base, the expert system must also possess an element which can scan facts and rules, and provide answers to the queries given to it by the user. This element is known as the inference engine. The inference engine has the ability to look through the knowledge base and apply the rules to the solution of a particular problem. It is, therefore, the driving force of the expert system.

The user interface is the means by which the user communicates with the expert system. Ideally this interface should be as English-like as possible so as to facilitate use by inexperienced users. That is, an ideal expert system would allow the user to type (or speak) his questions to the system in English. The system would then recognise the meaning of the questions, and use its inference engine to apply the rules in the knowledge base to deduce an answer. This answer would then be communicated back to the user in simple English.

Such an ideal system is, however, not likely to be available in the immediate future due to the difficulties which arise in trying to program a computer to recognise, and understand the meaning of, even the most simple English sentences and phrases.

1.3 Applications

Expert systems are becoming more widely used in many fields of business, commerce and industry. It is, however, true to say that it is only in very recent times that businessmen and industrialists have begun to realise the potential of such systems to improve the efficiency and competitiveness of their operations. For this reason, there are still relatively few examples available of well tried and tested expert systems. Indeed, the majority of people involved in expert systems are in the research and development area and have not yet produced fully operational systems. There are, however, a small number of well established expert systems, some of which were developed as early as the 1970s.

It is the purpose of this section to give the reader a brief overview of some of the application areas in which expert system technology has been found to be effective.

1.3.1 Early systems

As mentioned above, some of the earliest expert systems were developed during the 1970s. These included one of the most well known and well documented systems, namely MYCIN. MYCIN is an expert system which was designed at Stanford University to deal with problems in the treatment and diagnosis of infectious diseases. The system, therefore, comprises a large knowledge base which contains facts and rules about the forms and causes of infectious diseases and can thus be used to aid the clinician in his diagnosis. Another system which was developed around the same period as MYCIN is PROSPECTOR, which was designed by SRI International in association with the United States Geological Survey, to assist geologists during mineral exploration work. Both of these early expert systems contain large amounts of knowledge which have been drawn from well understood and researched problem domains.

1.3.2 Social applications

In recent years, there has been a large amount of research into the social applications of expert systems; that is, systems which can be used to improve both the quality and quantity of advice and expertise available to the man in the street - a sort of computerised Citizen's Advice Bureau. Systems which are currently available and/or under development include:

a large Alvey project (see Section 1.4.2) which aims to computerise the legislation and practice relating to social security benefits a system which is designed to advise expectant mothers as to their maternity rights, including knowledge about eligibility for maternity benefit, maternity pay etc.

a system, currently available on a microcomputer, which gives advice on an employee's rights with respect to dismissal, redundancy pay, etc.

an expert system which is designed to give home owners advice on planning law and answer such questions as "Is my plan for an extension likely to be approved?".

One could imagine how such systems could be made available to the general public in such places as libraries, large indoor shopping precincts, etc. In addition, future developments in microcomputer and television technology could make such expert systems even more accessible, by providing their facilities on your own television screen.

1.3.3 Financial applications

Expert systems are also in current use in many large financial institutions such as insurance companies, banks and finance houses. The type of systems which are in common use include:

expert systems which aid bank managers when they are deciding whether or not to grant a loan to a particular customer

systems which give advice as to whether to grant a mortgage or not

systems which advise insurance companies as to the risk factor involved in insuring a particular individual or item

systems which are used by credit card companies to help them decide whether or not to issue an individual with a credit card

1.3.4 Industrial applications

Many industrial and manufacturing companies have now introduced expert systems into their daily operations. Applications in this area include:

expert systems which are capable of diagnosing various industrial faults, such as faults in aircraft, gas turbines and helicopters

an expert alarm system which is designed to minimise plant downtime and avoid shutdowns, by identifying any potential problems as rapidly as possible

expert systems which are used to design and machine small mechanical parts (such systems may form part of a much wider plant automation system which may also utilise robots)

military applications of expert systems such as the identification of targets and potential threats to security

1.3.5 Summary

This section has outlined just a few of the numerous applications of expert systems. It is hoped, therefore, that it has succeeded in giving the reader a "feel" for the current uses of expert systems and, also, their potential for the future. There are also many very good texts which are devoted entirely to the topic of expert systems and their applications. For the interested reader who wishes to research this area further these texts are listed in the bibliography at the end of this book.

1.4 Initiatives in the expert systems area

This section aims to discuss two recent initiatives in the expert systems area, namely the Japanese Fifth Generation Project and the United Kingdom's Alvey programme (and, in particular, its Intelligent Knowledge Based Systems component).

1.4.1 The Japanese Fifth Generation Project

It is generally accepted that the history of computer hardware can be divided into four generations, stretching from the inception of computers in the mid-1940s to the present day. These four generations are each described below.

The first generation of computers emerged in the mid-1940s. These were extremely large, valve-based machines which were so vast that they filled an entire room and needed several people to operate and look after them.

In the mid-1950s advances in electronics resulted in the valve being largely superseded by the much smaller transistor. This enabled computer manufacturers to construct what was to become known as the second generation computer which was a much more compact, transistor-based machine.

Further advances in electronics during the mid-1960s enabled component manufacturers to combine entire circuits on a single device. These devices were known as integrated circuits (IC's). The use of IC's in the production of computers heralded the advent of the third generation computer, which was , once again, much more compact than its direct predecessor.

In the early 1970s another new age dawned with the mass production of much more powerful IC's. Each of these IC's contained a much larger amount of circuitry, and a corresponding larger number of individual components. This new technology was known as Large Scale Integration (LSI) and the resultant devices were termed "chips". The fourth generation of computers thus consisted of machines which were constructed entirely of such chips and were, once again, much more compact than previous models. It was also around this period that the first microcomputers began to appear.

So what is a Fifth Generation computer?

In 1981 the Japanese announced the Fifth Generation Computer Project, whose aim is to produce machines which will form the next generation of computer systems. However, unlike the previous four generations of computers, the fifth generation machine is not envisaged as being purely a result of advances in computer hardware. Rather, the vision of the fifth generation computer is that of a computer system which not only utilises the full gamut of recent advances in both hardware and software technologies, but also embodies a radical new approach to the very philosophy behind the function and architecture of a computer system.

All of the previous generations of computers have been essentially data processing and/or number crunching engines. In order to use such machines, the operator has had to program the computer with an appropriate method of solution to the problem in hand. The philosophy behind the fifth generation computer is that the user will be able to communicate with the machine in natural language (e.g. English) and that the computer will contain sufficient knowledge to be able to understand and solve his problems. The fifth generation computer will thus be a highly sophisticated and powerful knowledge processing and problem solving machine consisting of a vast knowledge base, a powerful inference engine and an extremely friendly and intelligent user-interface system.

The system will, by necessity, utilise each of the following recent advances in computer technology:

parallel processing - in order to provide the powerful knowledge processing and problem solving capabilities, the computer will consist of many processors each executing in parallel. Each of these processors will be searching one portion of the knowledge base, or solving one particular part of the entire problem currently in hand.

Very Large Scale Integration (VLSI) - in order to provide such vast processing power and parallel processing capabilities the fifth generation computer will make full use of the latest advances in VLSI - the ability to store extremely large numbers of components and circuits on a single chip.

logic programming - much of the software for the fifth generation computer will be written in a logic programming (or Artificial Intelligence) language such as Prolog or Lisp. Such languages are capable of expressing facts and rules and can be used in the construction of the powerful inference engines which will be required.

intelligent interfaces - it is envisaged that the system will be extremely easy to use. It will recognise not only natural language typed in at the keyboard, but will be able to understand continuous speech and will also have computer vision capabilities.

Basically what the Japanese are attempting to produce is a system which resembles, as closely as possible, a human being in its intelligence and knowledge. However, the system will be even more powerful in its problem solving capabilities than any human being could ever hope to be. The system will also be extremely easy to use - ideally the user will be able to speak his problem to the computer in his own native tongue.

Such a computer system is obviously a bold leap from the systems which are currently available. It is, therefore, expected to take at least a decade for the current research and development work in the fifth generation field to reach anything near fruition.

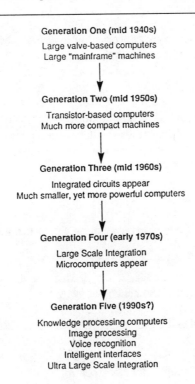

Fig 1.2

1.4.2 The ALVEY Programme

The ALVEY programme of advanced Information Technology (IT) research is a joint venture between the British Government, British industry and academia. It is a five year programme which began in 1983 and was mounted largely as a response to the

Japanese Fifth Generation initiative.

The prime objective of the ALVEY programme is to develop the British IT industry through a programme of collaborative projects. The program is named after John Alvey, who was chairman of the committee which recommended that such a venture should be undertaken.

The ALVEY programme is divided into five major areas:

> Very Large Scale Integration (VLSI)
> Software Engineering
> Intelligent Knowledge Based Systems (IKBS)
> Man-Machine Interface (MMI)
> Systems Architecture

It is with the IKBS area that we are concerned in this section, for it is this area which has included a large amount of research in the expert systems field. An IKBS is, like an expert system, a computer system which embodies knowledge and expertise about a particular problem domain.

The IKBS component of the ALVEY programme comprises four large projects known as "demonstrator" projects and numerous smaller research projects. It has also resulted in the formation of several ALVEY clubs which have been set up to discuss and research various aspects of IKBS.

The four demonstrator projects involve:

> the development of an expert system to aid in the formulation of chemical mixtures

> the use of IKBS techniques in the production of mechanical systems (in particular diesel engines and helicopter gearboxes)

> the development of a decision support system for aircrews and a flight-deck simulator

> the use of IKBS techniques for stock control

In addition the ALVEY programme has established four "large- scale" demonstrator projects which are intended to draw from several of the five main components of the programme (including, of course, IKBS). Each of these projects involves substantial IKBS work. The projects include:

> the development of an expert system which will embody current knowledge relating to social security benefit legislation and practice

the production of a speech-input word processor and accompanying fifth generation workstation

the development of a "design support system" which will be used to aid designers throughout all stages of product development, from initial design through to manufacture

The IKBS component of the ALVEY programme is, thus, using the above projects and many others to push forward the boundaries of expert systems technology in many different application areas.

1.4.3 Summary

This section has presented an overview of two important initiatives which relate to the expert systems field. There are , however, many other current research projects in the expert systems area. The interested reader may wish to explore this area further by referring to some of the texts listed in the bibliography at the end of this book.

1.5 The future

It is a very difficult, but none the less, exciting task to speculate about the future possibilities that artificial intelligence and expert systems may offer to the computing industry and to the public in general. One thing is, however, certain : they are unlikely to go away! Indeed, it is quite possible that the field of AI is one of the most promising advances in technology that the world has ever seen.

The computing or information technology industry is, in comparison with such established industries as engineering, relatively immature. That is, there is no long history behind the computing industry. The methods, techniques and concepts which are being applied in computing are themselves not yet fully tried and tested . Yet the industry is growing at an amazingly rapid rate - much more rapidly than the rate at which any earlier industrial revolutions have developed. It is for this reason that theory and research are perhaps rather far ahead of practical use.

This situation will not continue for ever, however. As previously stated, the world of commerce and industry is beginning to wake up to the potential that artificial intelligence has to offer. Some of the more obvious opportunities which are currently available (and are being exploited to varying degrees) are discussed briefly below.

The use of robots is creeping into many industrial plants. We have all seen such robots on television, perhaps being used to construct or paint a car in a modern plant. This application of AI technology will, without doubt, spread into all areas of engineering and the "hard" construction" industry in addition to areas such as laboratory automation.

Work on computer vision, speech recognition and natural language understanding will, when it has reached fruition, produce computers which possess most of the senses of a human being. The extent to which these "senses" will be able to be developed, however, remains to be seen. The next stage would be to transplant these senses within a robot, to thus produce a machine which can see us, hear us , understand us and talk back to us! All of this may seem like something out of a science fiction film; however, stranger things have happened!

The future of expert systems themselves is perhaps even more assured than that of the remainder of AI. This is because expert systems are already being put to practical use in many fields of human endeavour (as covered in Section 1.3 of this chapter). The breadth of usage of expert sytems is bound to expand so that such systems are used to simulate human expertise in all areas of life, both at home and at work. Indeed, it is perhaps in the home where we will see some of the greatest and more obvious applications of expert systems. Expert systems could be used for gaining advice on such subjects as legal problems, house purchasing and extension planning from the comfort of your own home. These systems could be available at the touch of a button at a home terminal connected via a telephone line to national or international networks of such facilities.

Chapter 2

Expert System Development

2.1 Which problem areas are best suited to expert system treatment?

As we have learnt in the previous chapter, expert systems are gradually finding their way into many areas of modern life. So should we expect to see expert systems appearing in every office, shop and factory in the near future? Perhaps not. Indeed, only certain types of application are suited to implementation in expert system form. But how do you determine whether or not a particular problem area is suitable for the "expert systems" treatment? It is the aim of this section to answer this question.

The following rules give an indication of the sort of criteria which must be satisfied in order for a particular application area to benefit from expert system treatment:

> The field under study should be able to be reduced into a series of rules rather than mathematical formulae or equations. In particular, expert system treatment is not applicable if the problem involves a large number of calculations.

> The field under study should be well understood so that well-defined rules can be formulated to represent human expertise.

> The field under study should not encompass problems which take too short (i.e. less than half an hour) or too long a time to solve (a long time meaning longer than, say, one week.)

> There should be general agreement among recognised experts in the field (i.e. it is no use if all the experts have different ideas or theories - in such a case whose knowledge would you computerise?).

> The number of rules necessary to describe the system should be sufficiently large to warrant the development of an expert system (say, more than about a dozen rules - for less it is probably more efficient to solve the problem manually).

> There should be one or more "tame" experts who are agreeable to their involvement in the project.

Notwithstanding the above rules, however, any application that requires access to specialist expertise is a potential area for the introduction of expert systems technology.

But what exactly are the benefits that can be gained by the introduction of an expert system?

There are many benefits that can accrue from the introduction of expert systems technology within a particular application area. Some of the more obvious benefits include:

> expert systems can make knowledge and expertise much more accessible than would otherwise be possible

> expert systems can be much more cost-effective (i.e. much cheaper) than hiring the services of a real human expert

> expert systems are not prone to human error in the application of their rules

> expert systems can be used to facilitate communication between experts themselves and hence improve their own expertise.

Having decided that a particular problem domain is suitable for expert systems treatment, and that it will be beneficial to introduce such a system, the most obvious question which one might ask is:

> How do we go about developing an expert system?

The next section of this chapter aims to answer this question.

2.2 Knowledge engineering

Knowledge engineering is the (currently fashionable) buzzword which is used to describe the process of extracting knowledge about a particular problem area from an expert (or group of experts). Although this process is commonly referred to as knowledge engineering, it does, in fact, comprise two distinct stages. It is the second of these two stages which is, strictly speaking, the knowledge engineering phase. The two stages are:

> knowledge acquisition (or elicitation) - the process of acquiring the knowledge from the expert(s)

> knowledge engineering - the process of formulating (or engineering) the knowledge into a form suitable for expression in an AI language such as Prolog.

Throughout this section, however, the term knowledge engineering will be used to refer to the whole process (that is, both of the above stages).

The knowledge engineering process can be compared to that of the conventional systems analyst whose job is to analyse an existing manual or computerised system with a view to designing a new computerised system to improve efficiency, productivity and/or performance. But, where the systems analyst is involved in the flow of information within a particular system, the knowledge engineer is interested in the organisation of knowledge and how it is applied to the solution of problems.

The knowledge engineer must, therefore, be able to somehow obtain from his tame expert(s) the necessary facts, rules and skills and convert them into a form suitable for expression in an appropriate language. This, as you might imagine, is not a simple task.

To start with, an expert may be far from tame! He may be hostile to the idea of a stranger coming along to "steal" his knowledge and expertise only to implant it in a computer system which may (as he perceives the situation) eventually replace him altogether. Also, even if the expert is totally in agreement with the idea of computerising his knowledge, he may find it difficult to express in words those skills, judgments and (often) "gut feelings" which have become second nature to him.

The knowledge engineer can take several possible approaches to surmount this problem. One widely used technique involves getting the expert to work his way through a few carefully chosen sample problems. From observing the manner in which the expert approaches and solves these problems, the knowledge engineer can then deduce the rules which the expert is intuitively applying. Other techniques involve interviewing the expert over several sittings, asking questions which will force him to explain the manner in which he applies his particular specialism.

Some knowledge engineers prefer to become a "fly on the wall" and use a video camera to record the expert doing his everyday work over a suitable period of time. The resultant video tapes are then examined at a later date and the relevant knowledge and expertise extracted.

Having obtained the basic concepts of knowledge, the knowledge engineer must then rearrange the knowledge into:

> facts about the problem domain

> rules which can be used to make inferences from the facts and information provided by the user.

For example, consider the following scenario which describes a simple area of expertise:

John Russell is an expert in grading students' examination answers. He takes his work very seriously, but on being questioned by a knowledge engineer it is obvious that his method of marking an examination answer follows a definite set of rules.

John explains that the questions which he marks always have essay type answers. His method of marking an answer involves reading the essay and marking a red line in the margin for every good (i.e. relevant) point which he spots. He then totals up the red marks which he has made in the margin of the student's answer book. If a student has less than four red marks it is obvious that that student has not answered the question very well. However, in such cases John will read the essay again to see if it does marginally answer the question and is hence worthy of a pass. If it does he awards a bare pass, which is a C grade; otherwise he awards a fail (F) grade. If a student has between four and six red marks in the margin John awards a B grade. If a student has more than six red marks he is awarded an A grade, which is equivalent to a merit.

The process which John Russell follows in grading his students' answers can be expressed by the following simple "knowledge base":

Rules:

>IF number of marks < 4 AND essay does not answer question
>THEN award grade F
>
>IF number of marks < 4 AND essay does answer question
>THEN award grade C
>
>IF 3 < number of marks < 7
>THEN award grade B
>
>IF number of marks > 6
>THEN award grade A

Facts:

>Grade A is a MERIT
>
>Grade B is a PASS
>
>Grade C is a BARE PASS
>
>Grade F is a FAIL

The above simple example demonstrates how the process of grading examination answers can be translated into a series of simple rules and facts. It is the job of the knowledge engineer to undertake the process of acquiring knowledge and transforming it into such facts and rules. He will, of course, be dealing with much more complex areas of human expertise, which may eventually reduce to tens or even hundreds of rules.

Because the concept of expert systems is relatively new, the knowledge engineer is also a relatively new individual. For this reason, the skills and techniques required to perform the knowledge engineering process are understood fully only by that small select group of individuals who have seized the opportunity to throw themselves into this new and exciting area.

You will not find any college courses or degrees in knowledge engineering; nor will you see all your friends changing jobs from programming or systems analysis to knowledge engineering. There are, however, a small number of commercial companies who offer short courses in knowledge engineering and this area is one which is sure to expand in the future.

2.3 Expert system design - the role of Prolog

The end result of the knowledge engineering exercise is a series of facts and rules describing the relationships between objects within a particular problem domain. In order to express this "knowledge base" in a form suitable for input to a computer, it is necessary to translate these facts and rules into a programming language. The majority of existing computer programming languages are, however, designed to deal with character or numeric data in the following traditional manner:

accept input data

process this data to produce the required output

print (or display) the results.

Such languages as this are termed procedural languages because they are designed to perform step by step procedures on the input data. Common procedural languages are BASIC, FORTRAN, COBOL, Pascal and Ada.

Procedural languages depend on the programmer to find a method of solution to his problem as a series of steps and express this method of solution in the statements provided by the language. These statements are limited by the way in which the electronic components of the computer hardware operate and therefore consist of basic operations such as printing, reading, adding and subtracting, etc. This form of language is of little or no use in the field of expert systems where the approach needs to be entirely different. In the construction of expert systems we need to be able to:

set up a knowledge base consisting of facts and rules about a particular problem area be able to ask questions of the expert system without worrying about how the computer system will provide an answer. That is, the expert system must have within it an inference engine which is capable of inferring solutions to the user's queries from the facts and rules embedded in the knowledge base.

The sort of language requirements needed to satisfy this type of situation are:

the language must be able to express facts and rules in terms of relationships between objects in the problem domain

the language must be "declarative" as opposed to procedural.

A declarative (or non-procedural) language is a language which allows the user to express "what" a problem is without worrying about "how" a solution to that problem is to be obtained. That is, the user simply has to express clearly and unambiguously the elements of a problem and the language itself will be able to provide a solution. A declarative language thus allows the user to express the "what" of a problem without having to figure out "how" to solve it. Prolog is such a language.

It is for this reason that Prolog has been chosen by the Japanese as the main language for the development of much of the software for their fifth generation computer system. The remainder of this book is devoted to coverage of the Prolog language and its applications in the field of expert systems.

Chapter 3

Introduction to Prolog

3.1 The Prolog environment

Prolog provides the user with a total environment consisting of facilities for the rapid development of expert systems. This environment is interactive and conversational; that is, it allows the user to sit at the computer terminal and take part in a conversation with Prolog. This conversation session will usually begin with the user entering facts and rules about a particular problem area, thus defining an expert system for that area. Alternatively, the user may ask Prolog to load an already existing expert system which he wishes to use. The user will then ask Prolog a series of questions (known as queries) relating to the particular problem area from which the system draws its expertise. Prolog will then respond by providing answers to these queries.

A Prolog program takes the form of a database of knowledge (a knowledge base) about a particular problem area. The terms database (of knowledge), knowledge base and program are thus (arguably) interchangeable in the context of the Prolog language.

To enter the Prolog environment you must first obtain access to the computer system and then type in the appropriate command to enter the Prolog environment. This command is usually simply

```
prolog
```

You will then receive the standard Prolog "query" prompt which is instantly recognisable:

```
?-
```

The query prompt is simply informing you that Prolog is waiting for you to ask it a question. In fact, Prolog can be thought of as a question-and-answer environment which is continually waiting for you to ask it queries about those subjects for which it has been given knowledge and expertise. The questions which you ask Prolog must always be phrased in lower case letters. This important point is worth stressing at the earliest possible stage as uppercase (capital) letters have a special meaning in Prolog (this will be explained later).

The query prompt signifies that you are in query mode. This is the mode which allows you to ask questions of the database of knowledge which is currently available to

27

Prolog. The system also provides one other mode which is known as "consult" mode. Consult mode instructs Prolog to "consult" files containing knowledge in the form of Prolog rules and facts. The operation of consult mode is explained in detail in the next section.

The command needed to leave the Prolog environment will depend upon the particular computer on which you are working and the version of Prolog which you are using. In general, however, this command will be the standard exit command for your system (this is CTRL Z on DEC systems).

3.2 Entering a simple knowledge base - facts

The simplest way in which we can give knowledge to Prolog is in the form of a collection of facts. These facts must be expressed in the correct manner according to the grammar rules, or syntax, of Prolog. For example, consider the following simple English fact:

Mary wears a dress.

This fact consists of two important components:-

a relationship

objects

In this particular fact the relationship is "wearing" and it is used to relate together two objects; a person (Mary) and the dress. The fact would be expressed in Prolog as

```
wears(mary,dress).
```

Notice that the Prolog fact consists of the name of the relationship followed by the name of the two objects enclosed in brackets. In Prolog terminology the relationship is known as a *predicate* and the objects are known as *arguments*. The entire fact is known as a clause. Notice also that the names of both the relationship and the objects are expressed in lower case and that the clause is terminated by a full stop. The latter point is a very important one to remember as Prolog uses the full stop to recognise the end of a fact. It is very easy to miss out your full stops from a Prolog program - the results of doing so can be both annoying and disastrous.

The order of the two arguments mary and dress within the brackets does not have any significance to Prolog. However, it is important that the user is consistent in the way in which he orders arguments within a particular program. For instance, the two facts

```
The dog bites the man
```
and
```
The man bites the dog
```

are obviously very different and this must be reflected in their translation into Prolog by using consistent ordering of the arguments as below

$$\text{bites(dog, man)} \quad \text{--- The dog bites the man}$$

$$\text{bites(man, dog)} \quad \text{--- The man bites the dog}$$

It should also be noted that the existence of one of the above facts within the database does not imply the existence of the other fact. That is, the fact that the dog bites the man does not imply that the man bites the dog!

Here are some more simple Prolog facts.

fact	meaning
count(dracula).	Dracula is a count.
prince(charles).	Charles is a prince.
gardener(james).	James is a gardener.
married(jane,david).	Jane and David are married.
friends(tony,peter).	Tony and Peter are friends.
drinks(joyce,coffee).	Joyce drinks coffee.
drive(john,pauline,bmw).	John and Pauline drive a bmw.

Notice that facts may have any number of arguments, depending upon the number of objects which you wish to relate together. For instance; the predicate count has one argument; the predicate friends has two arguments and the predicate drive has three arguments. It should also be stressed that Prolog has no means of knowing whether or not the facts which you give are true. For example, the fact

$$\text{bird(pig).} \quad \text{(A pig is a kind of bird)}$$

is perfectly acceptable to Prolog.

Now let us set up a simple knowledge base comprising facts about a particular scenario. Consider the following hypothetical situation which consists of a series of facts about the items of clothing which a group of people wear to a party.

```
Mary wears a dress.
Tina wears trousers.
Fred wears a suit.
Terry wears a suit.
Tina wears a red blouse.
Fred wears a white shirt.
Terry wears a blue shirt.
```

In order to enter the above scenario as a series of seven Prolog facts you must first enter consult mode. This is achieved by typing

```
[user].
```

after the   ?- query prompt.

This command is telling Prolog that you wish to consult a database that you, the user, will enter at the terminal.

You will then be presented with the consult prompt:

```
|
```

You can then enter the appropriate Prolog facts, namely (and remember not to forget the full stop at the end of each fact):

```
|  wears(mary,dress).
|  wears(tina,trousers).
|  wears(fred,suit).
|  wears(terry,suit).
|  wears(tina,red_blouse).
|  wears(fred,white_shirt).
|  wears(terry,blue_shirt).
```

and leave consult mode by typing the standard exit command for your own particular system (this is CTRL Z on DEC systems). You will then be automatically returned to query mode.   CTRL XC

Notice in the database of facts which you have entered the underscore character (_) has been used to string two words together to form a single Prolog object.

You can then use query mode to ask Prolog questions about the clothes which particular individuals were wearing to the party. For instance, you may wish to ask

```
Was Mary wearing a dress ?
```

This could be done by typing

```
?- wears(mary,dress).
```

In order to respond to the above query Prolog will examine the database looking for facts which match the question. A fact matches a question if its predicate and arguments are spelt the same and the arguments are in the same order. As our simple knowledge base does contain such a fact Prolog will find a match and will provide you with the response

```
yes
```

However, if you were to ask Prolog whether Mary was wearing green shoes by typing

```
?- wears(mary,green_shoes).
```

no matching fact would be found in the database and Prolog would give the response

```
no.
```

This is,of course, not to say that Mary was not wearing green shoes but only that Prolog is not aware of such a fact because the current knowledge base does not contain any such information.

When we give Prolog a query to answer we are setting it a "goal" to achieve. In other words, in asking the question

```
?- wears(fred,suit).
```

we are setting Prolog the goal of proving that Fred was wearing a suit to the party. In this case the answer would be yes and the goal is said to succeed. If, however, we ask Prolog the question

```
?- wears(tim,red_tie).
```

hence setting the goal of proving that Tim was wearing a red tie to the party, Prolog will reply no and the goal is said to fail.

The concept of goals and their success or failure is one of the most fundamental and important ideas in Prolog. Indeed, the Prolog system is designed to continually try and satisfy goals in order to provide answers to queries given to it by the user.

3.3 Variables

A variable is used when it is possible for a particular structure to have one of several different values. For instance, the database which was discussed in the previous section of this chapter contained information about various items of clothing worn to a party by different people. We might, therefore, wish to ask a question such as

What items of clothing did Tina wear?

The above query would be expressed

```
?- wears(tina,Clothing).
```

where Clothing is a variable name and begins with an uppercase (capital) letter. In general, variables must begin with a capital letter and consist of letters, digits or underscore characters.

In order to find an answer to the above question Prolog would attempt to find a match in the database. This it would do when it came across the second fact in the database,

```
wears(tina,trousers).
```

The result of this match is that the variable Clothing would take the value "trousers" and Prolog would thus respond

```
Clothing = trousers?
```

This, of course, is not the only answer to the query. Indeed, the question mark is signifying the fact that Prolog is asking us if we wish to search for any further solutions. We can tell Prolog to search for more answers by typing

```
;
```

immediately after Prolog has given us the first answer. The entire question-and-answer session would thus appear:

```
?- wears(tina,Clothing).
Clothing = trousers? ;
Clothing = red_blouse? ;
no
```

If you do not wish Prolog to search for any more answers to your question you simply press the return key after you have been given the first answer. The system will then return to query mode as shown below:

```
?- wears(mary,Clothing).
Clothing = dress? < return >
yes

?-
```

In general, matching a variable which does not currently have a value with an object sets the variable to the value of that object. A variable which does not have a value is known as an "uninstantiated" variable. When it is matched with an object it is "instantiated" (set) to the value of that object. For example, the result of matching

```
white(X)
```

with

```
white(rolls_royce)
```

32

is that the previously uninstantiated variable X is instantiated to the object "rolls_royce".

3.4 Conjunctions

In this section we will move on to the means of forming more complex goals for Prolog to satisfy.Consider the program below which contains information about students at a college:

```
male(tim).
male(marc).                    --- male(X) succeeds if X is male.
male(simon).

female(louise).
female(hazel).                 --- female(X) succeeds if X is female.
female(marie).

year(tim,4).
year(marc,1).
year(simon,2).                 --- year(X,Y) succeeds if the student
year(louise,3).                X is in year Y of his/her course.
year(hazel,1).
year(marie,4).

studies(tim,history).
studies(marc,philosophy).
studies(simon,mathematics).    --- studies(X,Y) succeeds if the
studies(louise,computer_science).   student X studies subject Y
studies(hazel,chemistry)
studies(marie,art).

age(tim,24).
age(marc,18).
age(simon,25).                 --- age(X,Y) succeeds if
age(louise,21).                X is Y years old
age(hazel,22).
age(marie,32).
```

The sort of question which one might wish to ask Prolog about such a knowledge base could be:

Do any male students study history?

In order to express the above question in Prolog it is necessary to form a more complex query than those which have been dealt with so far in this chapter. This is because the question involves the use of two forms of fact from the knowledge base:

- those facts which state which students are male
- those facts which state which subject a student studies

We have,therefore, to join two simple queries together with the "and" symbol, which is denoted by a comma. The correct form for this particular query would thus be

```
?- male(X),studies(X,history).
```

which translates literally to

Is there an X who is male and studies history?

This is what is known as a conjunction of goals. We are giving Prolog a goal to satisfy which consists of a conjunction (joining) of two goals, namely

```
male(X)
```

and

```
studies(X,history).
```

In order to satisfy the complete goal Prolog must first satisfy these two subgoals. If it cannot find a value for X which will satisfy both subgoals the complete goal will fail (and Prolog will answer no). Of course, in this particular case the response would be

```
X = tim?
```

An even more complex query of this knowledge base might be

Does any first year student who is older than 20 study chemistry?

which is expressed as a conjunction of subgoals in the form

```
?- year(X,1),age(X,Y),Y>20,studies(X,chemistry).
```

and produces the response

```
X = hazel?
```

Notice that we have introduced the greater than symbol in the goal $Y > 20$. This goal succeeds if the value of Y is greater than 20. The treatment of numbers, and the use of such operators as $>$ is discussed in greater detail in Section 6.1 of this book.

3.5 Blank variables

If we are not interested in the value of a particular variable in a question we can use the blank (or anonymous) variable. This is signified by a single underscore (_) character. For instance, if we wished to use our knowledge base about the college students from the previous section to answer the question:

Is there a male student who studies philosophy?

and we did not wish to know the name of the student in question, we would phrase the query

```
?- male(_),studies(_,philosophy).
```

to which Prolog would simply reply yes.

3.6 Syntax rules

Syntax rules are those rules relating to punctuation, spelling, etc. that we are forced to adhere to in order to produce correct Prolog programs. The use of incorrect syntax in our Prolog programs will result in error messages and programs that will not work. It will then be necessary to use the editor to correct the errors.

The following points concerning Prolog syntax are worth restating as they provide some of the commonest mistakes in Prolog programming

The full stop - the full stop is used to denote the end of a clause. Prolog will take everything between two full stops as a single clause. Thus, if you do forget a full stop after a clause, Prolog will run that clause into the next and will continue to do so until it does encounter a full stop. It will then become confused as to what this strange new clause means and signal its displeasure by giving you an error message.

Lower case letters - these must be used as the first character of the names of objects and predicates. For example, apple, pear, likes, male, female.

Uppercase (capital) letters - These are used as the first character of variable names. For example; Mother, Father.

Arguments - the arguments of a predicate must be enclosed in round brackets and separated by commas. For example, parents(john,Mother,Father).

The comma (,) - this means "and" and is used to join two or more goals to form a conjunction of goals.

The semicolon (;) - this means "or" and, during a question- and-answer session, is used to ask Prolog to search for another answer to your question. It can, however, also be used to form what is known as a "disjunction" of goals. For instance, the query

```
?- drives(mick,car);rides(mick,bicycle).
```

means

> Does Mick drive a car OR ride a bicycle?

This goal will succeed if either of the two subgoals drives(mick,car) or rides(mick,bicycle) succeeds. In general, however, it is not considered good practice to use the ; symbol too frequently within your Prolog programs as it can make the logic of them unclear and difficult to follow.

The underscore symbol (_) - this can be used within object, variable or predicate names to join together two or more words. For example red_car, ginger_beer, Mother_in_law. Remember also that a single underscore character denotes the anonymous (or blank) variable.

3.7 Exercises

1. Express the following English facts in Prolog.

(a) Tony likes swimming.
(b) A Rolls Royce is a large, expensive car.
(c) Dogs chase cats.
(d) Alison flies a plane.
(e) Harry is tall.
(f) Susan has friends Terry, Elaine and Tracy.

2. Describe the following family tree as a series of Prolog facts.

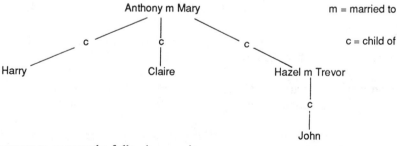

Use your program to answer the following queries.

(a) Who is the sister of Harry?

(b) Who is the brother of Hazel?
(c) Who is the father of John?
(d) Who is the mother of Claire?
(e) Who is married to whom?

Note: the questions which you ask will have a bearing on the way that you structure your facts.

3. Watsons Ltd. is a company which manufactures furniture. They require a system which will allow the owner of the Company, Mr. Watson, to access information about any of his employees when he requires it; for example, when working out who is due for promotion. Mr. Watson has nine employees at the moment. The company is organised in such a way that each employee has a person above him in the company known as a supervisor. The diagram below depicts all the employees and their supervisors:

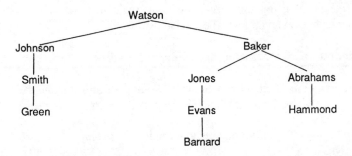

The supervisor of each employee is the person immediately above him in the diagram. So, for example, Watson is the supervisor of Johnson and Baker, Johnson is the supervisor of Smith, and so on.

Write a Prolog program which contains all the supervisor relationships shown in the above diagram.

Express the following queries in Prolog, and find their solutions.

     (a) Is Johnson the supervisor of Smith?
     (b) Is Abrahams the supervisor of Jones?
     (c) Who is the supervisor of Evans?
     (d) Who does Baker supervise?
     (e) Who supervises whom?
     (f) Does anyone supervise Johnson?

3.8 Notes for Turbo Prolog programmers

3.8.1 The Turbo Prolog environment

Turbo Prolog is a compiled version of the Prolog language which is produced and marketed by Borland International Inc. and is designed to run on IBM PC microcomputers and their compatibles. Because Turbo Prolog is a compiler rather than an interpreter (as are most versions of Prolog) the programs which it produces are extremely rapid in terms of execution time. This is the case because a compiler translates the whole of the program into executable form before running, whereas an interpreter translates the program instruction-by-instruction as it runs.

Turbo Prolog provides the user with an extremely friendly environment for the development of his software. This environment is a menu-driven system which contains full editing and debugging (error finding) facilities.

On entering Turbo Prolog you are presented with the main menu which consists of four "windows" in which text can appear. These windows are:

the editor window - used for entering and editing programs

the dialog window - this is the window in which your programs run and the conversations which you have with Turbo Prolog appear

the message window - Turbo Prolog uses this window to display messages to the user

the trace window - this is used for "tracing" what happens during execution of your program. This is particularly useful when debugging your program and is explained in more detail in Section 5.6.

The main menu also provides you with a set of commands to choose from, written across the top of the screen. These commands are:

```
Run Compile Edit Options Files Setup Quit
```

You select one of these commands by typing the first letter of its name or by moving the highlighted bar over it (using the arrow keys) and then pressing the return key.

In order to enter a Turbo Prolog program you must choose the Edit option from the main menu. You can then type a program into the editor window. The commands for use within the editor are explained fully in the Turbo Prolog manual and are summarised at the bottom of the page when you are in the edit mode.

Once you have finished typing in your program you must press the escape key to leave the editor and select the Run option from the main menu to run your program. The dialogue relating to your program will then appear in the dialog window.

3.8.2 The structure of a Turbo Prolog program

Although Turbo Prolog is based on Prolog (and is, in fact, a superset of the language) the structure of a Turbo Prolog program is somewhat different from that of a "standard" Prolog program. In general, a Turbo Prolog program has the following basic structure:

domains   domain statements

predicates   predicate statements

goal   this section may or may not appear and consists of the goal to be satisfied by the program.

clauses   this section consists of the Prolog clauses (this part of the program is that which you would find in "standard" Prolog)

We will now consider each of the above sections in detail.

domains - the domains section specifies the "domains" to which the objects within your program may belong. The objects which have been considered in this chapter have belonged either to the symbol or the integer domain. For example, the program in Section 3.4 would have a domains section as below.

```
domains
      person,subject = symbol
      age_year,college_year = integer
```

predicates - this section is used to define the predicates to be used in your program. It specifies the names of the predicates, their arguments and to which domain these arguments belong. For instance, the program in Section 3.4 would have a predicates section as below.

```
predicates
      male(person)
      female(person)
      year(person,college_year)
      studies(person,subject)
      age(person,age_year)
```

The domain and predicate sections are included in the Turbo Prolog language to provide extra checks on your program for you and hence help you to produce more reliable software. For instance, if you were to type the goal

```
male(5).
```

Turbo Prolog would respond with the message

```
type error
```

because you have defined that the predicate male must have an argument which is a symbol, and not an integer. Standard Prolog would not have this extra check built into it and would, therefore, not identify the above mistake as an error. Instead it would simply reply no.

goal - this section is used to specify the goal to be satisfied when the program is executed. That is, instead of entering a series of goals when you run the program, as is the case in Standard Prolog, you can specify exactly what you wish the program to achieve within the program itself. This means that if you wish the program always to satisfy the same goal you may specify that goal within this section. For example, the program in Section 3.4 might have a goal section

```
goal
        male(X),studies(X,history).
```

During execution the program would, therefore, provide an answer to this "query" and this query alone. If no goal is specified within your program (that is, the goal section is omitted), Turbo Prolog will ask for a goal (query) when the program is executed with the prompt

```
Goal:
```

in the dialog window. Note that the ?- prompt and, therefore, the concept of consult and query mode do not exist in Turbo Prolog.

clauses - this section is identical to that which you would expect to find in a standard Prolog program and contains the clauses which make up the "knowledge base" of your Turbo Prolog program.

3.8.3 A sample Turbo Prolog program

Consider the program in Section 3.4 as it would appear in Turbo Prolog. This is shown on the next page:

```
domains
        person,subject = symbol
        age_year,college_year = integer

predicates
        male(person)
        female(person)
        year(person,college_year)
        studies(person,subject)
        age(person,age_year)

clauses
        male(tim).
        male(marc).
        male(simon).

        female(louise).
        female(hazel).
        female(marie).

        year(tim,4).
        year(marc,1).
        year(simon,2).
        year(louise,3).
        year(hazel,1).
        year(marie,4).

        studies(tim,history).
        studies(marc,philosophy).
        studies(simon,mathematics).
        studies(louise,computer_science).
        studies(hazel,chemistry).
        studies(marie,art).

        age(tim,24).
        age(marc,18).
        age(simon,25).
        age(louise,21).
        age(hazel,22).
        age(marie,32).
```

3.8.4 Running and saving a Turbo Prolog program

In order to run (execute) a program you must select the Run option from the main menu. If Turbo Prolog detects any syntax errors within your program when it attempts to run it you will be thrown back into the editor and the cursor will flash at the point where the error lies in your program. You can thus remove the error immediately and then rerun your program.

Assuming that your program has been compiled correctly it will now attempt to satisfy the goal which has been specified in the goal section of the program. If no goal has been specified it will display the

        Goal:

prompt in the dialog window. You can then enter a goal (i.e. a "query") as described in the body of this chapter. If the goal succeeds Turbo Prolog will respond with the message

        True

otherwise it will respond with the message

        False

Notice that the words True and False replace yes and no.

If there is more than one solution to a goal you will be automatically provided with all of the solutions. That is, Turbo Prolog does not prompt you for a semi-colon (;) to ask if you wish it to find any further solutions.

The terminal session below illustrates the output produced in the dialog window when the program in Section 3.8.3 is run.

```
Goal: age(X,Y).
        X=tim,   Y=24
        X=marc,  Y=18
        X=simon, Y=25
        X=louise, Y=21
        X=hazel, Y= 22
        X=marie, Y=32
        6 Solutions
        Goal: age(tim,24).
        True
        Goal: age(tim,35).
        False
        Goal:
```

To save your program on disc you must select the Files option from the main menu. You will then be presented with the files menu from which you will have to choose the Save option. You will then be prompted to enter the name of the file in which you wish your program to be stored.

To exit from the Turbo Prolog environment you must select the Quit option from the main menu.

Chapter 4

More Complex Programs

4.1 Consulting files

So far we have loaded information into Prolog via consult mode. That is, we have typed our knowledge base of facts while sitting at the terminal. Such knowledge bases are only available for our use while we are in the Prolog environment and are lost on exiting from Prolog. This is obviously not a very productive way of working, to say the least! It would seem more sensible to be able to prepare knowledge bases prior to entering the Prolog environment and then consult these from within Prolog. Such knowledge bases would be permanently stored on disc and could thus be used at any time in the future. In order to do this you must create and name a disc file and use an editor to type your Prolog program into it. The majority of versions of Prolog provide their own editing facilities which allow you to prepare and save programs from within Prolog. Your computer system will also have its own system editor and this could also be used to store your program in a disc file. Whichever editor you prefer to use, the important thing is that you are creating a permanently stored version of your program.

After typing in and saving your program you can consult it in a similar manner to that which you used to enter consult mode. That is, you simply type

```
?- [filename].
```

where filename is the name of the file to be consulted. Prolog will then load the program in that file into its database, ready for you to ask queries of it.

It is also possible to consult a series of files by placing their names one after each other in the square brackets. For example, the command

```
?- [data,'b:expert',example].
```

would instruct Prolog to consult three files; data, b:expert and example. Notice that the second filename in the list is enclosed in single quotes. This is because the : symbol within its filename would confuse Prolog. Prolog would tell you that it had successfully consulted the files by replying

```
data consulted
b:expert consulted
example consulted
yes
```

43

It should be noted that the programs contained in the three files are stored in the database in the order in which they are consulted. That is, the program contained in the file named data would be stored at the head of the database with the programs contained in b:expert and example beneath it. The order in which such information is stored in the database can be very important as we shall discover later when we come to discuss the way in which Prolog searches through its database.

Similarly, any files which are subsequently consulted during a session will be stored at the bottom of the current database.

4.2 Rules

So far in this book we have considered databases which consist solely of one form of clause; namely the fact. There is one other important form of clause which is known as the rule. In order to develop Prolog programs which are of any real practical use it is necessary to use rules.

In our programs so far Prolog has had a comparatively easy task to perform in finding answers to our queries. This is because our programs have been comprised of nothing more complicated than a collection of facts. In order to answer a question, therefore, Prolog has simply had to find a fact which provides an exact match to the query. But the language also has very powerful facilities for making inferences from rules expressed in the knowledge base. It is the structure of rules and the method which Prolog uses when searching them that we will explore next.

Let us start by considering a simple rule

```
eats(john,Y):- food(Y),
               sweet(Y).
```

which states that John eats a commodity Y provided that Y is a food and Y is sweet. The above rule consists of three important elements (as do all Prolog rules):

the head of the rule (in this case eats(john,Y))

the :- symbol (which can be read as "provided" or "if")

the body of the rule (in this case food(Y),sweet(Y)).

Prolog uses rules in the following manner. When we give Prolog a query we are, as we know, setting it a goal which can either succeed (if a match for the query is found), or fail (if no match is found within the database). If a fact which matches the query exactly (that is its predicate and arguments match and its arguments are in the same order) is found then Prolog immediately records a success and returns the appropriate answer(s). If, during its search of the database, Prolog comes upon a rule which may provide a match it proceeds in the following manner:

first it attempts to match the query with the head of the rule. If such a match is achieved, then the goal will succeed if the goals which form the body of the rule succeed.

The goals which form the body of the rule are known as subgoals and, in the example above, the body of the rule consists of a conjunction of two subgoals food(Y) and sweet(Y).

Prolog has thus reduced the task of trying to satisfy a query such as

```
?- eats(john,Y).
```

to that of satisfying two subgoals:

```
food(Y)
```
and
```
sweet(Y).
```

Prolog will thus search the database in an attempt to satisfy these two subgoals. If it does so (that is, the two subgoals succeed) then the goal which forms the head of the rule will also, by inference, succeed and hence Prolog will provide us with an answer to our query.

Now let's turn this rather general example to a more specific one by examining a complete program which includes the eats rule which we have just considered.

```
eats(john,Y):- food(Y),
               sweet(Y).

food(grapefruit).
food(biscuit).
food(lemon).
food(apple).
food(orange).
food(cake).
food(meat_pie).
food(jelly).

sweet(biscuit).
sweet(orange).
sweet(cake).
sweet(jelly).

bitter(lemon).
bitter(grapefruit).
bitter(beer).
```

Consider how Prolog would deal with the following query

```
?- eats(john,biscuit).
```

This query sets Prolog the task of proving that John eats biscuits. In order to satisfy the above goal Prolog would search for a match in the database. This it would find when it encountered the head of the eats rule because the predicate (eats) and the arguments (john and biscuit) will match, with the variable Y in the head of the eats rule being instantiated to the value "biscuit". At the same time all the other occurrences of the variable Y within the eats rule are also instantiated to "biscuit". This is because the variable Y is said to be "sharing" within that rule. When one occurrence of a shared variable is instantiated to a particular value all other occurrences of that variable within the same clause are also instantiated to the same value.

So the goal has now been reduced to that of satisfying the conjunction of subgoals

```
food(biscuit),sweet(biscuit).
```

In order to satisfy this conjunction of subgoals Prolog must find a match to both food(biscuit) and sweet(biscuit). It will succeed in doing this as both of these facts are present within the database. These two subgoals will thus be satisfied and the entire rule will, therefore, also succeed and Prolog will provide a positive response to the query.

Consider, however, the query

```
?- eats(john,meat_pie).
```

This reduces to the task of satisfying the conjunction of subgoals

```
food(meat_pie),sweet(meat_pie).
```

Although a match would be found for the first subgoal food(meat_pie) no match would be found for the second subgoal sweet(meat_pie), which would fail. This failure would result in the failure of the entire goal and Prolog would thus reply no.

Consider the following queries and the responses which Prolog provides.

```
?- eats(john,cake).
yes

?- eats(john,_).
yes

?- eats(john,lemon).
no
```

```
?- eats(john,X).
X = biscuit ? ;
X = orange ? ;
X = cake ? ;
X = jelly ? ;
no

?- eats(fred,cake).
no
```

Think carefully about the above question-and-answer session and make sure that you understand how, and why, Prolog arrived at the above answers. Type the database into your own computer system and try the session for yourself.

4.3 Comments and other points on formatting your programs.

When writing your Prolog programs it is worth spending a little extra time to ensure that your programs are both readable and comprehensible. It is easy to convince yourself that, because you understand a program fully when you are designing it, you will also be able to understand it at any time in the future. This is by no means true. It is more likely that, when you return to the program at some point in the future, you will find it exceedingly difficult to figure out the point of the program and how it works. This is even more the case for someone else who wishes to understand what your program is doing and how it does it.

4.3.1 Comments

There are a few simple measures which you can take to ensure that your programs are comprehensible to yourself and others. This will mean that, if it is necessary to modify your programs at any time in the future, the task of doing so will be made much more simple and straightforward.

The first measure which you can take to make your Prolog programs more readable and comprehensible to both yourself and other users is to sprinkle it liberally with comments. A comment is enclosed in the symbols /* and */ as below. % -TO4

```
/* This is a comment */

/* Comments can stretch over more than one line
if necessary - as long as they are enclosed
in the correct symbols */
```

It is difficult to give general rules as to when and where comments should be used

47

within programs. However, the following points are worth mentioning:

A general comment at the beginning of a program is a good idea. Such a comment should explain the purpose of the program and could include other details such as who developed the program, when it was developed and for whose use it was designed.

It is good practice to place a comment beside each set of clauses of a similar form. For an example of this, have a look at the program in the next section.

Remember that, for someone reading a program for the first time, there is no way of knowing whether

```
likes(peter,marie).
```

expresses the fact that Peter likes Marie or the fact that Marie likes Peter. (Remember also that these are two quite different facts and that one definitely does not imply the other!) It is, therefore, sensible to include comments to prevent such ambiguities.

Whilst we are on the subject of how to make your programs more comprehensible, it is worth mentioning two other measures which can be taken to improve the readability of your programs.

4.3.2 Formatting rules

When typing in a rule, it is useful if you structure it in the following format:

```
head:- subgoal1,
       subgoal2,
       subgoal3,
       subgoal4.
```

That is, place each subgoal on a separate line under each other, and indent the subgoals with respect to the head of the rule. This will make your rules easier to pick out and read at first glance.

4.3.3 Meaningful names

The readability of your programs can be greatly improved by using meaningful names for your predicates, objects and variables. That is, try not to use variable names such as X and Y, which bear no meaning whatsoever, but choose some names that describe exactly what your variables represent, such as Father and Mother, for example. Remember you can use the underscore character (_) to string words together in names (for instance white_car, bitter_lemon).

4.4 An example knowledge base

At this point it is useful to consider a complete Prolog program.

```
/* Sample knowledge base which describes the
relationships between a group of people */

male(john).
male(fred).            /* john, fred and harry are male */
male(harry).

female(mary).
female(julie).         /* mary, julie, susan and anne */
female(susan).         /* are female */
female(anne).

blonde(john).
dark(fred).            /* john has blonde hair while */
dark(harry).           /* fred and harry have dark hair */

brunette(mary).
blonde(julie).         /* julie and susan are blonde */
blonde(susan).         /* mary and anne are brunette */
brunette(anne).

/* The rules below describe who likes who.
The predicate likes(X,Y) succeeds if the
person X likes the person Y */.

likes(john,Person):- female(Person),
                     blonde(Person),
                     rich(Person).

likes(fred,Person):- female(Person),
                     brunette(Person).

likes(harry,Person):- female(Person),
                      rich(Person).

likes(mary,Person),:- male(Person),
                      dark(Person).

likes(julie,Person):- male(Person),
                      dark(Person),
                      rich(Person).
```

```
/* A person is rich if he owns gold */

rich(Person) :- owns(Person,gold).

owns(fred,gold).
owns(john,car).          /* facts about, who owns what */
owns(julie,gold).
owns(anne,house).
```

The following question-and-answer session relates to the above program. Study it carefully as it acts as an illustration of the Prolog facilities covered so far.

Prolog code	Explanation
`?- male(X).`	Who is male?
`X = john ? ;`	John
`X = fred ? ;`	Fred
`X = harry ? ;`	Harry
`no`	no other males
`?- likes(john,X).`	Who does John like?
`X = julie ? ;`	Julie
`no`	no-one else
`?- likes(mary,Z).`	Who does Mary like?
`Z = fred ? ;`	Fred
`Z = harry ? ;`	Harry
`no`	no-one else
`?- likes(julie,_).`	Does Julie like anyone?
`yes`	yes
`?- likes(X,Y),likes(Y,X).`	Is there a couple who like each other?
`X = fred`	
`Y = mary ?`	Fred and Mary
`yes`	

4.5 Definitions

In this chapter and the previous one we have met a number of new terms and concepts, each of which is vital to the understanding of Prolog. As the chapters which follow will build upon the foundations laid here, it is sensible to pause for a moment and review the definitions that we have met so far.

Clause - a clause is a fact or rule within a Prolog database.

Goal - when we give Prolog a query to answer we are setting it a goal to satisfy. If it can find a match in the database the goal will succeed; otherwise it fails.

Instantiation - Prolog terminology for setting a variable to a particular value. A variable which is not defined (does not yet have a value) is said to be "uninstantiated". A variable which does have a value is said to be "instantiated".

Matching - Prolog attempts to find matches in the database to the queries which we set it. Two clauses are said to match if they have the same predicate and arguments and the arguments are in the same order. An uninstantiated variable will match with an object and the variable will become instantiated to the value of that object.

Object - a Prolog constant value. For example, apple, orange and pear are all objects. Object names begin with a lower case letter.

It is, however, possible to begin an object name with an uppercase letter by enclosing the name in single quotes, such as 'Frankenstein', 'Thomas' and 'Danube'. Similarly, special characters (including blanks) may be included in an object name by the use of single quotes; for example, 'New York', 'bye?' and '£5300'.

Predicate - the name of a clause in the database. A predicate has arguments which must be enclosed in brackets and are separated by commas.

Program - a Prolog program takes the form of a series of clauses (facts and rules). These form a database of knowledge (or knowledge base) about a particular problem area.

Rules - a rule consists of a head and a body. The head is the goal to be satisfied. This is reduced to the satisfaction of a conjunction of subgoals which form the body of the rule.

Sharing - variables within a clause which have the same name are said to be sharing. If one of these variables is instantiated to a particular value then the variables which are sharing with it are also instantiated to the same value.

4.6 Exercises

1. Rewrite the family tree program in Section 3.7, exercise 2 using rules as well as facts. Your program should, however, contain the same amount of information. Use your program to answer the same queries as before.

2. An employer is sifting through a large pile of applications which he has received for a recently advertised job vacancy. In order to produce a short list of candidates for interview he applies the following criteria:

51

In order to be selected for interview an applicant must be able to type and drive and must live in London.

(a) Express the employer's selection criteria as a Prolog rule.
(b) Express the following applicant details as Prolog facts:

John Smith lives in Cambridge, can drive but can't type.
Charles Brown lives in London, can drive and can type.
Mary Jones lives in Glasgow, can't drive but can type.
Tony Evans lives in London, can drive and can type.
Alice Green lives in Luton, can drive and can type.

(c) Ask Prolog to provide you with a list of applicants for interview.

4.7 Notes for Turbo Prolog programmers

4.7.1 Loading files

There is no concept of consult and query mode as in Prolog. In order to load an existing data base it is necessary to choose the FILES option from the main menu. You will then be presented with the Files menu from which you will need to choose the Load option. You will then be prompted for a file name. Turbo Prolog will then load the named file ready for you to run.

4.7.2 Points of syntax

The symbol :- and the comma (,) are replaced by the words "if" and "and" respectively in Turbo Prolog. However, for consistency with other versions of Prolog the Turbo Prolog compiler will also accept the :- and , symbols. For example, the eats rule in Section 4.2 could be written in Turbo Prolog in the more English-like form

```
eats(John,Y) if food(Y)
          and sweet(Y).
```

Turbo Prolog does not allow the use of single quotes to create complex object names. That is, objects such as 'King Canute' and 'London' are not allowed.

Chapter 5

Searching the Knowledge Base

5.1 Pattern matching

In order to develop more complex Prolog programs it is necessary to understand the process which Prolog follows when attempting to find answers to the questions which you set it. The sort of goals which we have been setting Prolog so far in this book have been of two different types. They have been:

goals which result in either a positive (yes) or negative (no) response

goals which, if satisfied, result in a value of a variable being supplied

We shall now consider, in detail, how Prolog arrives at a correct response in each of these two cases.

5.1.1 Simple queries which will result in a yes or no response

The sort of query which falls into this particular category is one such as

Does Terry drive a blue ford?

or, in Prolog terminology,

```
?- drives(terry,blue_ford).
```

In order to provide you with an answer to the above question Prolog must perform what is known as "pattern matching". That is, Prolog will search through the knowledge base until it finds an exact match to the goal which you have set it. The match will be exact only if the predicate of the goal is the same as one in the knowledge base, if it has the same number of arguments, and if these arguments are spelt the same and in the same order. Prolog performs its search by starting at the top of the knowledge base and working through the facts and rules in the knowledge base from left to right and top to bottom. The Prolog "inference engine" will thus work through all the Prolog code in the knowledge base until it finds a match, as illustrated in Figure 5.1.

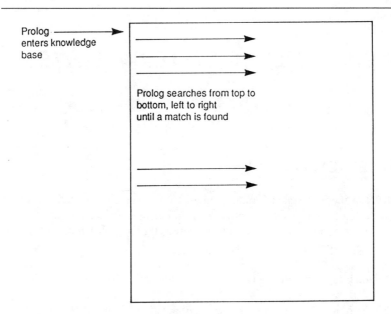

Prolog enters knowledge base

Prolog searches from top to bottom, left to right until a match is found

Fig. 5.1

If a match is found then Prolog will reply yes , otherwise it will reply no . Notice that in order to provide a negative response Prolog will have scanned every line of code (i.e. every fact and rule) in the current knowledge base. This may take a little time, depending upon the size of the knowledge base.

The discussion above assumes that a direct pattern match is found with a fact in the knowledge base. However, it may be the case that Prolog finds a match with the head of a rule in the knowledge base. For instance, in its search through the knowledge base, Prolog might encounter the rule

```
drives(Person,Object)  :- owns(Person,Object),
                          car(Object),
                          driver(Person).
```

```
/* a Person drives an Object if that Person owns
   that Object and that Object is a car and that
   Person is a driver */
```

As we know, the effect of matching the goal

```
drives(terry,blue_ford)
```

with the head of the rule

```
drives(Person,Object)
```

54

is that the variables Person and Object are instantiated to the values terry and blue_ford respectively. In turn, this results in the task being broken down into that of satisfying the conjunction of three subgoals which form the right hand side (i.e. the body) of the drives rule

```
owns(terry,blue_ford),
car(blue_ford),
driver(terry).
```

Prolog will now attempt to satisfy the above three subgoals in turn, working from left to right. It will not proceed to the next goal on the right until it has satisfied its neighbour on the left. That is, first it will attempt to find a match for the goal

```
owns(terry,blue_ford).
```

In order to do this it will again enter the knowledge base at the top and work through from left to right, top to bottom, until it finds an appropriate match. When it does so, Prolog will move to the next subgoal

```
car(blue_ford).
```

It will, once again, enter the knowledge base at the top and search through until it finds an appropriate match. Finally, when matches have been found for the above two subgoals, Prolog will attempt to find a match for the third and final goal in the conjunction, namely

```
driver(terry).
```

This will entail re-entering the knowledge base and searching for a suitable match. Only when it has satisfied this final subgoal (and thus the original goal) will Prolog be able to provide the customary yes as a response.

As you will have gathered, Prolog is relentless in its capacity for searching until it finds an answer, or it is satisfied that there is no (positive) answer to be found. It is continually entering and re-entering the knowledge base in its search, looking for a fact, or the head of a rule, which provides a direct match for its current goal.

5.1.2 Queries which result in a value of a variable being supplied as a response

The second type of goal which you might set Prolog is one which will result in more than just a yes or no response. In other words, you are asking it to provide you with a possible value for a variable. Such a goal might be

Does John drive a car ?

or, in Prolog terminology,

```
?- drives(john,Car).
```

The procedure which Prolog follows in order to provide you with a response is identical to that described in the previous section. That is, once again Prolog is relentless in its search for a solution, scanning the knowledge base until it discovers either a fact such as

```
drives(john,white_bmw).
```

in which case the answer

```
Car = white_bmw?
```

would result or the goal matches with the head of a rule such as we had previously:

```
drives(Person,Object)  :- owns(Person,Object),
                          car(Object),
                          driver(Person).
```

In this case the variable Person will be instantiated to the value john and the two uninstantiated variables Car and Object will match (and will, therefore, be in effect sharing). That is, the initial goal will be reduced to that of satisfying the conjunction of subgoals

```
owns(john,Object),
car(Object),
driver(john).
```

where the variable Object is synonymous with the variable Car in the initial query (and hence when Object becomes instantiated to a particular value, Car will also be instantiated to the same value). Prolog will, therefore, re-enter the knowledge base in search of a fact or rule to match the first of the three goals in the conjunction, namely

```
owns(john,Object).
```

This it might find with a fact such as

```
owns(john,red_porsche).
```

Having discovered this fact, the variable Object will be instantiated to the value red_porsche throughout the conjunction of subgoals and Prolog will re-enter the knowledge base in an attempt to satisfy the goal

```
car(red_porsche).
```

If a match is found for this goal, Prolog will re-enter the knowledge base in an attempt to satisfy the final subgoal in the conjunction, namely:

```
driver(john).
```

Only when this goal is satisfied will Prolog respond with the answer

```
Car = red_porsche?
```

We can then either accept this answer as that which was required or we can type in the customary ; to instruct Prolog to resume its search to see whether or not John drives any other cars.

5.2 Backtracking

The description of Prolog's powerful pattern matching capabilities in the previous section omitted to explain what is one of the most important mechanisms available in Prolog. This mechanism is known as backtracking.

When searching for an answer to a question, particularly if obtaining the answer involves the use of rules and the subsequent satisfaction of conjunctions of subgoals, Prolog makes a series of choices as to which values it instantiates variables to. Basically, because of the top to bottom, left to right manner in which Prolog searches through the knowledge base, it will choose the first possible match which it discovers. This match might not, however, be the one which is required in order to provide a satisfactory solution to the problem in hand. That is, Prolog might find that subsequent goals will fail as a result of having made the wrong choices at an earlier stage. Backtracking is the mechanism by which Prolog can go back and make other choices for the values of variables and then attempt to resatisfy subsequent goals. This is best illustrated by an example program.

Consider the following program which is based upon the example in the previous section of this chapter:

```
drives(Person,Object)  :- owns(Person,Object),
                          car(Object),
                          driver(Person).

driver(john).
driver(sarah).
driver(tony).
sailor(fred).
pedestrian(malcolm).
```

```
owns(fred,yacht).
owns(john,bmw).
owns(tony,raleigh).
owns(sarah,raleigh).
owns(tony,ford).

car(bmw).
bicycle(raleigh).
car(ford).
boat(yacht).
```

Consider that you give Prolog the query

```
?- drives(tony,Car).
```

The first match that Prolog will find will be the head of the rule at the top of the knowledge base. This will result in the variable Person in the rule being instantiated to the value tony and the variable Car in the query sharing with the variable Object in the rule. This reduces the problem to that of satisfying the conjunction of subgoals

```
owns(tony,Object),
car(Object),
driver(tony).
```

Prolog will thus re-enter the knowledge base in an attempt to find a match for the goal

```
owns(tony,Object).
```

The first match which it will encounter (remember that it is searching from top to bottom) will be

```
owns(tony,raleigh).
```

This will result in the variable Object being instantiated to the value raleigh throughout the conjunction of subgoals. Prolog will then move to the next (second) goal in the conjunction, that is

```
car(raleigh).
```

and will attempt to find a match in order to satisfy this subgoal. This attempt will fail - Prolog will search the knowledge base from top to bottom without finding a suitable match. It is at this point that Prolog must retrace its steps and "rethink" that which it has previously done. Prolog will backtrack to the last choice (instantiation) which it made; namely choosing the fact that tony owns a raleigh. It (Prolog, that is) is saying at this point, "My first choice was no use as it did not provide me with an answer - it led me to a dead-end later on. Let's go back and make another choice and see whether or not that helps me to obtain a solution to my problem."

So Prolog then discovers the next owns fact which relates to tony, namely

        owns(tony,ford).

Prolog will then attempt to satisfy the remaining subgoals to the right with this new value for the variable Object. That is, it will attempt to satisfy the goal

        car(ford).

This goal will succeed as a matching fact exists within the knowledge base.

Finally an attempt will be made to satisfy the goal

        driver(tony).

and this, also, will succeed. The resultant response will thus be

        Car = ford ?

It is the powerful backtracking mechanism provided by Prolog which makes it such a useful problem-solving tool. Prolog will try every possible combination of choices in order to provide you with an answer to your query. Only when it has tried every possible combination and still failed will it be satisfied that no solution exists to your problem. It will then respond with the answer no.

In fact we have already met one way of instructing Prolog to perform backtracking. This is by the use of the semi-colon (;) in a question-and-answer session. When Prolog provides us with an answer to a query and we type in a semi-colon we are really saying to Prolog, "Go away and retrace your steps to see if there are any more possible answers to the question which I originally set you." Prolog, being our ever dutiful and tireless servant, does so gladly, and will continue to do so until there are no more possible new choices to make (and hence no more valid answers to our question) at which point it will inform you of this with a rather curt "no"!

How does Prolog manage to remember all the choices which it has previously made in order to retrace its steps so quickly?

It does so by placing a series of markers as it threads its way through a conjunction of goals. Each time it instantiates a variable to a particular value it leaves a marker which says, "I made a choice here. I shall mark it so that, if need be, I can return and undo that choice in order to choose another value." On backtracking Prolog will return to the last marker which it left and choose the next possible value for the variable which it instantiated at that point. It will then proceed to try to resatisfy subsequent goals. If it fails again it will again return to that marker and make yet another choice. This it will continue to do until either the subsequent goals succeed or there are no more choices to be made at the marked point. If the latter is true (i.e. it has exhausted all of the choices to be made at a particular marked point) Prolog will go back to the marker previous to that point and continue in a similar manner. It is in this manner that Prolog manages to cover all the possible combinations of values of variables which could possibly provide a solution to the problem which it has been set by the user.

5.3 The box model - debugging

5.3.1 Debugging

As the programs which you develop become more and more complex, the likelihood of their performing correctly the first time you run them decreases. That is, it is more and more likely that your programs will contain errors, or bugs as they are commonly known.

There are two main types of error with which we must concern ourselves. These are

syntax errors

logical errors

Syntax errors are, as discussed in Section 3.6 of this book, mistakes which have been made in the syntax of a Prolog program. That is, these are parts of a program which do not follow the grammatical rules of the Prolog language. These can, of course, have been caused by simple typing errors, such as

```
plays[tom,chess)
```

where a square bracket has been typed instead of a rounded bracket. Another very common syntax error in Prolog is caused when commas or full stops are omitted from their correct positions in the program. Prolog will notice these errors when we ask it to consult the program in question and will respond with an appropriate error message. This error message will, hopefully (and depending upon which particular version of Prolog you are using), enable you to locate the exact position of the syntax error within your program. All that then remains to be done to correct such an error is to enter the editor and retype the mistake.

Logical errors are, unfortunately, not so easy to detect, or rectify. A logical error occurs when the "logic" of your program is incorrect. That is, the rules and facts which constitute your program do not accurately reflect the problem in hand. Such errors may become all too obvious when you attempt to run your program and something unexpected occurs. This unexpected occurrence might be signified by the output of obviously incorrect answers or the production of a long string of answers when only one answer was required and expected. It is, however, quite possible that logical errors will go completely unnoticed, particularly if the answers which you are provided with by Prolog appear to be quite reasonable and plausible.

Debugging is the process of removing the errors from your program. It can be quite a tricky process, particularly if the program which is being developed is large and complex. In such cases it is wiser to develop your program as a set of smaller components, each of which can be tested and debugged separately.

In order to satisfy yourself that your program is functioning as you intended, it is necessary to test it by giving it sample queries which have been carefully chosen to try out, as far as possible, every potential path through the program. This ideal may not be possible in practice, as the number of paths through any reasonably sized Prolog program is likely to be infinite (this is particularly true if backtracking is likely to occur). It is, therefore, necessary to select test queries which will cover as many paths through the program as is possible in a reasonable amount of time. The subject of software testing is, in fact, quite complex and the interested reader would be well advised to consult one of the several texts on the subject.

5.3.2 The box model

It is often difficult to try and follow the path which Prolog takes in its relentless search for a solution to a particular query. This is particularly true if the search involves the use of backtracking to determine the various solutions to the problem in hand. It is, however, often desirable and, indeed, necessary to do so, particularly if, as discussed in the previous section of this chapter, the Prolog program is not producing the answers which you might have expected. In such a case you will need to trace the procedure which Prolog has followed to provide you with the sequence of answers. In such a way you can determine exactly where any problem lies and correct it. On the other hand, you may discover that the answers which Prolog has been giving you are, indeed, correct and that it is you who have been mistaken in expecting some other answers.

Prolog provides the user with a series of debugging predicates which allow you to trace the search which Prolog is making when it is executing your programs. The actual debugging facilities which are available are, however, very much dependent upon the particular version of Prolog which is available to you. One of the most common debugging systems is discussed in more detail in the following section.

Before considering these debugging predicates it will be helpful to consider a diagrammatic representation which is very useful when trying to describe the control flow of a Prolog program. This representation is commonly known as the 'box model'.

The box model imagines each Prolog predicate to be a box through which the flow of control of the Prolog interpreter passes. The box, which is depicted in Figure 5.2, has four entrance/exit "ports" one at each of the four corners of the box.

These ports are:

CALL - this is the port via which Prolog enters the box in order to try and satisfy a goal

EXIT - this is the port via which Prolog leaves the box having satisfied the goal (i.e. a success has occurred)

FAIL - this is the port via which Prolog exits the box if the goal has not been satisfied (i.e. a failure has occurred)

REDO - this is the port via which Prolog re-enters a box on backtracking in an attempt to resatisfy a particular goal.

Fig. 5.2

These four ports are placed in their particular corners of the box for a special reason, which is best illustrated by first considering an example.

Consider the Prolog predicate bird(X) below which succeeds provided the object X is a bird; where a bird is defined as an object which is covered in feathers and can fly. (As you will probably notice, this definition, and hence the program, is not strictly correct as there are several birds which cannot fly!)

```
bird(X)  :- covered(X,feathers),
            fly(X).

covered(hen,feathers).
covered(budgie,feathers).

fly(budgie).
walk(hen).
```

If we were to ask Prolog the query

```
?- bird(X).
```

the path through the program will be as illustrated in Figure 5.3. As you can see, the overall goal to be satisfied bird(X) is represented by the largest, outermost box (denoted Box A in Figure 5.3 and the description below) and the subgoals covered(X,feathers) and fly(X) are represented by boxes within this outermost box (denoted Boxes B and C respectively). The procedure which Prolog follows is as described below.

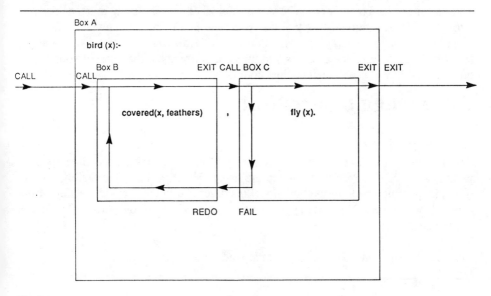

Fig. 5.3

The initial query causes a CALL of the bird(X) goal. This causes control to enter the CALL port of Box A. This CALL port is connected directly to the CALL port of Box B, which represents the covered(X,feathers) goal. Box B is, therefore, entered and the goal succeeds with the variable X being instantiated to the object hen . This success causes the flow of control to pass through the EXIT port of Box B which is connected to the CALL port of Box C, which represents the fly(X) goal. As X is instantiated to hen this corresponds to a CALL of the goal fly(hen) which, of course, fails as there is no match present within the knowledge base. The flow of control leaves Box C via, therefore, the FAIL port which is connected to the REDO port of Box B. Prolog is, at this point, backtracking to try and find another object which is covered in feathers. This it does, and X is instantiated to the object budgie . The flow of control then leaves Box B via the EXIT port. This in turn causes control to re-enter Box C via the CALL port. The goal which is to be satisfied at this point is fly(budgie). This goal succeeds and the flow of control leaves Box C via the EXIT port, and finally leaves the entire system of boxes via the EXIT port of BOX A. At this point the initial goal has been satisfied and Prolog responds with the output

```
X = budgie?
```

The above simple example serves to illustrate how each of the four ports of a box can be linked to the next (i.e preceding or succeeding) box in a chain of Prolog subgoals.

Similarly, a Prolog goal which consists of several subgoals is represented by a box with a series of boxes within it. The flow of control can pass from one box to the next and return to previous boxes if backtracking is necessary to determine a solution.

The concept of the box model can be very useful when you are trying to trace your way through a Prolog program. It is true that using the box model representation for large programs can involve many "boxes within boxes". However, it does serve as a useful tool which, at the very least, makes you think carefully about the logic of your Prolog program and how it is executed by your computer.

5.4 Debugging predicates

5.4.1 Spy/Trace

The debugging facilities available to you may differ considerably depending upon the particular version of Prolog which you are using. The most complete facility consists of a full implementation of the box model (as described in the previous section of this chapter) which prints a message whenever one of the four ports of a box is encountered.

This facility is obtained by typing the command

    spy.

after the ?- prompt and before running your program. (In some versions of Prolog the command is trace and not spy.)

The above command will place what is known as spy points on each of the predicates in your program so that, when it is executed, its progress though the box model can be reported to you. On executing your program Prolog will inform you as to which port of which particular box has been entered/exited. It will then wait for a response from you. Your response will instruct the Prolog debugger to perform one of several options which are available to you. These options are explained in detail in Section 5.4.2. If, however, you simply press the return key, Prolog will continue with its task of working through your program. To switch off the spy facility you simply type the command

    nospy.

The following terminal session illustrates the use of the spy facility as applied to the "bird" program in the previous section. (Remember that any text which is typed after the ?- prompt has been typed by the user - the rest of the terminal session has been supplied by Prolog.)

Notice that the debugger gives each successive Call a number in brackets. This number indicates the "depth" of Call (i.e. the number of Calls which have been made within the initial goal which is Call (1)). Notice also that variables are denoted by an underscore followed by a unique number. As this simple example program involves only a single variable X, this is denoted _1.

Terminal Session	Explanation
`?- ['bird.pl'].`	Consult file bird.pl which contains the bird program

`bird.pl consulted`
`yes`
`?- spy.`
	Place a spy point on each of the predicates in the program

`Spypoint placed on fly/1`
`Spypoint placed on walk/1`
`Spypoint placed on prolog_error/2`
`Spypoint placed on bird/1`
`Spypoint placed on covered/2`
`yes`
	Prolog tells you on which predicates it has placed spy points

`?- bird(X).`	Ask Prolog to find a bird

`** (1) Call :bird(_1)?`
`** (2) Call :covered(_1,feathers)?`
`** (2) Exit : covered(hen,feathers)?`
`** (3) Call : fly(hen)?`
`** (3) Fail : fly(hen)?`
`** (2) Redo : covered(hen,feathers)?`
`** (2) Exit : covered(budgie,feathers)?`
`** (4) Call : fly(budgie)?`
`** (4) Exit : fly(budgie)?`
`** (1) Exit : bird(budgie)?`
	Pressing Return after each line causes Prolog to step through the program using the box model

`X = budgie ? ;`	An answer is generated The ; tells Prolog to search for another answer

`** (1) Redo : bird(budgie)?`
`** (4) Redo : fly(budgie)?`
`** (4) Fail : fly(budgie)?`
`** (2) Redo : covered(budgie,feathers)?`
`** (2) Fail : covered(_1,feathers)?`
`** (1) Fail : bird(_1)?`
	Prolog backtracks but fails to find another answer

`no`	
`?- nospy.`	Remove the spy points

`Spypoint placed on covered/2 removed`
`Spypoint placed on bird/1 removed`
`Spypoint placed on prolog_error/2 removed`
`Spypoint placed on walk/1 removed`
`Spypoint placed on fly/1 removed`
`yes`	

You may also notice that a spy point is placed on a predicate prolog_error, which is not part of the bird program. This is, in fact, a system predicate which is present all of the time and is used by Prolog to produce error messages.

One final point that you may have noticed is that the debugger refers to each of the predicates by its name followed by a slash (/) symbol and an integer number. This number indicates the "arity" (number of arguments) of the predicate. For instance, the predicate fly, which has a single argument, is referred to as fly/1, whereas the predicate covered, which has two arguments, is referred to as covered/2.

5.4.2 Spy options

As stated previously, when using spy to trace the action of your Prolog program, there are various options which may be used to obtain additional information and/or exercise further control over the execution of the program. These options are activated by typing a single character after the ? prompt, which is issued by the debugger after it has reached one of the ports of the box model. The major options available are

Option	Explanation
return key	continue
c	continue
;	backtrack - go to REDO port of current goal
f	fail - go to FAIL port of current goal
r	retry - can be used at EXIT port of a goal to go to the CALL port of that goal
s	skip - can be used at the CALL port of a goal to tell the debugger to skip all prompts until the EXIT or FAIL port of the current goal is reached
o	switch debugging off
u	unleash - causes the debugger to print out a message at each port but not wait for any response from the user
l	listing - list all clauses for the current predicate
a	abort execution and return to the Prolog environment
e	exit from Prolog system altogether - this needs to be used with care as all your work will be lost!

5.4.3 Further debugging predicates

In addition to the spy facility described above, Prolog provides several other predicates which are designed to be used for debugging purposes. These are listed in brief below for reference purposes.

Debugging predicate	Explanation
spy X.	Places a spypoint on the predicate X where X is the name of a predicate
nospy X.	removes all spypoints on predicate X
unleash.	causes the debugger to print out a message at each port of the box model but not wait for a response from the user as to which option is to be exercised
leash.	causes previously unleashed spy points to be leashed and thus require a response from the user
debugging.	prints a list of currently active spy points and whether they are leashed
nodebug.	removes all spy points (like nospy)

5.5 Exercises

1. An elderly couple, who live in London, enjoy spending their weekends going for one day excursions by train. Each weekend they plan at least one trip working to the principle that the trip must not cost more than £20 per person and that the destination must be no more than 125 miles from London. A segment of the train timetable which they use to plan their trips is shown below.

Destination	Price(£)	Distance from London (miles)
Edinburgh	£55	405
Brighton	£12.50	53
Newcastle	£39	278
Luton	£14	32
Cambridge	£18	60
Reading	£8	40

Design a program which will generate a list of acceptable day trips for the couple.

Note. The Prolog symbol for "less than or equal to" is =< .

2. Use the spy predicate to trace the operation of the program you have designed in Exercise 1 above.

5.6 Notes for Turbo Prolog programmers

The backtracking capabilities of Turbo Prolog are identical to those described within the main body of this chapter. It should, however, be noted that Turbo Prolog will automatically provide you with all of the possible solutions to a given goal and that it is not, therefore, necessary to prompt it to backtrack (see Section 3.8).

The debugging facilities provided by Turbo Prolog are, however, somewhat different and are, therefore, summarised in the section which follows.

5.6.1 The trace facility

Turbo Prolog provides a trace facility to allow the user to follow the flow of control when his program is executed. In order to put a trace on a program it is necessary to insert what is known as a compiler directive at the very beginning of your program. This compiler directive consists of the word trace as illustrated in the following program

```
trace
domains
  name = symbol
  size = integer
predicates
  room(name,size)
clauses
  room(a,67).
  room(b,45).
  room(c,25).
  room(d,125).
```

The above program is designed to contain information about rooms in a building. Each room has a name (in this case a single letter) and a size (i.e. the maximum number of people which the room can comfortably hold). In order to run the program the Run command is chosen from the main menu. It is then necessary to enter the goal to be satisfied in the dialog window. Consider that we enter the goal

```
Goal: room(X,Y),Y>50.
```

in order to find all of the rooms that will hold more than 50 people.

The F10 key can then be used to single step through the program. The trace operates in the following manner.

In the editor window a flashing cursor indicates on your program code the particular clause which is currently under consideration. In this way you can actually observe Prolog working its way through the knowledge base from top to bottom. The trace window will also inform you as to which clause is currently under consideration.

The trace provided by Turbo Prolog is based upon the box model, but will output one of only three messages: CALL (call a particular goal), RETURN (return from a particular goal, after success or failure) and REDO (attempt to resatisfy a particular

68

goal i.e. backtrack).

The final output in the dialog window is of the form

```
X = a , Y = 67
X = d , Y = 125
2 Solutions.
```

Chapter 6

More Advanced Techniques

6.1 Arithmetic

Prolog was not designed to perform numerical calculations and should not be used for the development of programs which involve complicated calculations. There are other languages such as FORTRAN, Pascal and Ada which are much better suited to such applications. Indeed, arithmetic and calculation is one area of Prolog which varies depending upon which particular version of the language you are using. Some versions of Prolog provide only integer arithmetic and have no real number facilities at all. Such versions can not be used to perform any calculations which involve real numbers (i.e. numbers with decimal points and fractional parts). Nowadays, however, the majority of Prolog interpreters do offer real number facilities. It will be assumed in this text that real numbers are supported. If, however, this is not the case with the version of Prolog with which you are working there may be some differences in the way in which your computer treats the examples which are covered in this section. This is particularly true in the case of division. For instance, with real number arithmetic, the result of the calculation 5/2 will be 2.5 whereas with integer arithmetic the result would be 2.

As stated at the beginning of this section; if the primary function of a program is to perform calculations it is unlikely that Prolog will be a suitable language in which to develop the program. Arithmetic should only be used in Prolog programs where it is necessary to perform a few simple calculations as part of a more symbolically oriented computation.

6.1.1 Arithmetic operators

Prolog provides the user with a number of predefined operators which may be used to perform basic arithmetic calculations. These are:

+	addition
-	subtraction
*	multiplication
/	division
div	integer division
mod	remainder after integer division
is	causes evaluation of an expression

The following question-and-answer session illustrates the manner in which Prolog evaluates arithmetic expressions. Study the queries and Prolog's responses to them carefully and make sure that you understand how they have been arrived at.

```
?- Ans is 5 + 1.
Ans = 6 ?
yes

?- X is 3 - 2.
X = 1 ?
yes

?- Y is 5 * 4.
Y = 20 ?
yes

?-A is 5 / 2.
A = 2.5 ?
yes

?- A is 5 mod 2.
A = 1 ?
yes

?- W is 5 div 2.
W = 2 ?
yes

?- X is 5 + 3 - 2.
X = 6 ?
yes
```

The general form of a goal involving the is operator is

```
object is expression
```

where object is a simple Prolog object and expression is any valid arithmetic expression. When Prolog encounters such a goal the arithmetic expression is evaluated and the object on the left is instantiated to the result of that calculation. Prolog evaluates arithmetic expressions in the following manner:

all multiplications and divisions are of higher priority than additions and subtractions and are hence performed first

operations of equal priority are evaluated from left to right

parentheses (rounded brackets) may be used to alter the order of evaluation - expressions in parentheses will be evaluated first

Consider the following query which involves an arithmetic calculation:

```
?- X is 5 + 3 * 2 - 6 / 2.
```

In order to respond to the above query Prolog will first evaluate the expression 5 + 3 * 2 - 6 / 2. In order to do so, the multiplication 3 * 2 (as the leftmost high-priority operation) will be performed first forming the intermediate result

```
5 + 6 - 6 / 2.
```

The division 6 / 2 would then be performed (as the next high-priority operation) producing the intermediate result

```
5 + 6 - 3.
```

Prolog would then perform the remaining (lower priority) operations, working from left to right. The addition 5 + 6 would thus be performed first producing the intermediate result

```
11 - 3.
```

Finally, the subtraction 11 - 3 would be performed producing the final result 8. The is operator would then cause the object X to be instantiated to this result and the response

```
X = 8?
```

would be produced.

6.1.2 Comparing values

Prolog also provides the user with a number of operators for comparing arithmetic values. These are:

Operator	Meaning
X > Y	X is greater than Y
X < Y	X is less than Y
X >= Y	X is greater than or equal to Y
X =< Y	X is less than or equal to Y
X = Y	X equals Y
X \= Y	X is not equal to Y

6.1.3 Example program involving arithmetic

```
/* program to compute whether one person is
   older or younger than another */

older(X,Y) :- age(X,Years1),
              age(Y,Years2),
              Years1 > Years2.
```

```
/* person X is older than person Y if
   X is Years1 old, Y is Years2 old and
   Years1 > Years2   */

younger(X,Y)  :- age(X,Years1),
                 age(Y,Years2),
                 Years1 < Years2.

/* similar rule for X younger than Y */

age(fred,45).
age(doris,21).
age(marie,32).     /* age facts */
age(peter,30).
age(david,5).
age(ashleigh,12).
```

6.2 Recursion

One of the most important, and difficult, concepts to grasp in Prolog is that of recursion. Most substantial Prolog programs that you will meet will have some recursive rules in them. This is because recursion is the natural means of expressing things in Prolog.

Before we move on to consider the role of recursion in Prolog programs, it is useful to consider what, in plain English terms, recursion means.

A recursive definition is one which defines something in terms of itself.

The following two sections describe two simple mathematical functions which are defined naturally in recursive terms. These will serve as useful (and classic) examples of recursion. The derivation of the Prolog code for each of the two functions is also explained in detail.

6.2.1 Factorial

The factorial of a whole number (integer) is defined as the product of all the positive integers which precede it. The factorial of an integer is denoted by writing the integer with an exclamation mark (!) after it. That is:

$5! = 5 \times 4 \times 3 \times 2 \times 1$ (which is, of course, 120)

$3! = 3 \times 2 \times 1$ (which is 6)

$1! = 1$

In general terms, then

$$n! = n \times (n-1) \times (n-2) \times \text{- - - - - - -} \times 3 \times 2 \times 1$$

As you might have noticed, however, it is also true that the factorial of a given integer is equal to the result of multiplying that integer by the factorial of the integer which immediately precedes it. For example:

$$5! = 5 \times 4!$$

because

$$4! = 4 \times 3 \times 2 \times 1$$

It is this type of definition of the factorial function which is said to be recursive because it defines factorial in terms of itself.

In general, then, the factorial of any positive integer n is given by the following recursive definition:

$$n! = n \times (n-1)!$$

Let us examine this definition a little more closely. The definition is telling us that the factorial of a number n can be calculated by multiplying n by the factorial of the number which is one less than n. But how do we find the factorial of the number that is one less than n? Presumably we would have to calculate the factorial of the number that is two less than n, and in order to calculate that we would have to calculate the factorial of the number that is three less than n, and so on. At this point we might begin to think that this idea of recursion will cause us to go on and on for ever in a never-ending spiral. This is not the case. One important point to remember when dealing with recursive definitions is that they must always be accompanied by what is known as a stopping condition.

In this particular example the stopping condition is given by the factorial of one which is, of course, one. The complete definition is, therefore, given by

$$1! = 1 \text{ (the stopping condition)}$$

$$n! = n \times (n-1)! \text{(the recursive definition)}.$$

Now we can see that if we wish to calculate 5! we know that it is equal to 5 x 4! , where 4! = 4 x 3!, and 3! = 3 x 2!, and 2! = 2 x 1! , and 1! = 1 (the stopping condition). We can then retrace our steps and say that because 1! = 1   then   2! = 2 x 1 = 2 , therefore 3! = 3 x 2 = 6, therefore 4! = 4 x 6 = 24, therefore 5! = 5 x 24 = 120.

Now let us try to develop the Prolog code which will implement the factorial function.

First it is probably useful to remind ourselves of the definition

$$1! = 1 \text{ (the stopping condition)}$$

$$n! = n \times (n-1)! \text{ (the recursive definition).}$$

The above definition can be translated more or less directly into Prolog. We will implement it in the form of a predicate factorial(Number,Fact) which succeeds provided the factorial of the positive integer Number is given by the value Fact .

The stopping condition can, therefore, be written as the fact

```
factorial(1,1).
```

and the recursive definition of factorial can be translated into the recursive rule

```
factorial(Number,Fact)  :- Numb1 is Number - 1,
                           factorial(Numb1,Fact1),
                           Fact is Number * Fact1.
```

Notice that the rule is recursive because it is defined in terms of itself.

The above rule states that Fact is Number! provided that Numb1 is Number - 1 , Fact1 is Numb1! and Fact is Number x Fact1. To use our factorial program we would simply give Prolog a query such as

```
?- factorial(4,X)./* calculate 4! */
```

This would cause Prolog to enter the database searching for a match for the initial goal factorial(4,X). First it would come across the stopping condition which would not match with the initial goal. It would then encounter the recursive rule, and would match with the head of this rule. The variable Number would be instantiated to the value 4 and the uninstantiated variable Fact would share with the variable X. This would reduce the task to that of finding a match for the following conjunction of subgoals

```
Numb1 is 4 - 1,
factorial(Numb1,Fact1),         /* stage 0 */
Fact is 4 * Fact1.
```

(This and each of the following "stages" will be numbered for subsequent reference purposes.)

The first of the three subgoals in stage 0 would succeed with the value of the variable Numb1 becoming 3. The conjunction of subgoals would thus become

```
3 is 4 - 1,
factorial(3,Fact1),              /* stage 1 */
Fact is 4 * Fact1.
```

Prolog would then re-enter the database in an attempt to satisfy the goal factorial(3,Fact1). Once again it would encounter the stopping condition and once again this would not match with the current goal. It would, however, find a match with the recursive rule again. In a similar manner to before, this would result in the creation of a conjunction of subgoals of the form

```
2 is 3 - 1,
factorial(2,Fact1),              /* stage 2 */
Fact is 3 * Fact1.
```

to be satisfied. Again the second of these three subgoals would cause Prolog to re-enter the database in the search for a match. Again a match would be found with the recursive rule and a conjunction of subgoals of the form

```
1 is 2 - 1,
factorial(1,Fact1),              /* stage 3 */
Fact is 2 * Fact1.
```

would result. At this point Prolog would re-enter the database in the search for a match for the goal factorial(1,Fact1). This time the goal would match with the stopping condition

```
factorial(1,1).
```

and no new subgoals would be created. Prolog would, therefore, return to stage 3 above with the value of the variable Fact1 at that stage instantiated to 1. It would then try to satisfy the final goal of the three goals in stage 3, namely

```
Fact is 2 * 1.
```

which it would do, resulting in the value of the variable Fact being instantiated to 2. But, of course, the three subgoals of stage 3 were created as a result of an attempt to satisfy the second of the three subgoals in stage 2. So Prolog would now return to stage 2 with the value of the variable Fact1 at that stage instantiated to 2. It would then try to satisfy the final goal of the three goals in stage 2, namely

```
Fact is 3 * 2.
```

which it would do, resulting in the value of the variable Fact being instantiated to 6. This, in turn would cause Prolog to return to stage 1 with the value of the variable Fact1 at that stage instantiated to 6. It would then try to satisfy the final goal of the three subgoals in stage 1, namely

```
Fact is 4 * 6.
```

This it would do and the variable Fact would be instantiated to the value 24. As all goals have now been satisfied Prolog would respond with the answer

```
X = 24?
```

Notice that the recursive rule fact will continually recreate itself until the stopping condition is reached. Prolog will then retrace its steps in order to provide the user with the final result.

Notice also that it is important that the stopping condition should appear above the recursive rule in the knowledge base. This is important because if this were not the case the stopping condition may never be found. If the recursive rule were to appear first in the knowledge base, this would be encountered first when Prolog re-entered the knowledge base and, as long as a match occurred, the stopping condition would never be reached, even when it should be. This would cause what is known as infinite recursion to occur which would probably cause your terminal to "hang up" and display nothing for several minutes before finally displaying an error message.

6.2.2 The Fibonacci sequence

The Fibonacci sequence of numbers is a sequence of positive integers such that the next number in the sequence is obtained by adding together the two previous numbers. The first two numbers in the sequence are both 1. The sequence is thus

1 1 2 3 5 8 13 21 34 55 . . . .

$F_1 = 1$

(two stopping conditions)

$F_2 = 1$

$F_n = F_{n-1} + F_{n-2}$ $n >= 3$ (recursive rule)

The above two stopping conditions are simply stating that the first term and the second term of the sequence are both equal to 1. The recursive rule is stating that, in general, the nth term of the sequence is obtained by adding together the two terms which immediately preceded it in the sequence (i.e the (n-1)th and the (n-2)th terms). That is, to obtain the fifth term (5) you would add together the fourth and third terms (3 and 2 respectively).

Once again, this will translate in a straightforward manner to Prolog:

```
fib(1,1).
fib(2,1).              /* two stopping conditions */
```

```
fib(Number,Term)  :- Numb1 is Number - 1,
                     Numb2 is Number - 2,
                     fib(Numb1,Term1),
                     fib(Numb2,Term2),
                     Term is Term1 + Term2.
```

/* recursive rule */

Notice that the fib rule is "doubly recursive" in that it consists of two recursive calls of itself. Thus two stopping conditions are required to halt the recursion (one for each of the two recursive calls). These two stopping conditions will be used when an attempt to compute the first two terms of the sequence is made.

6.2.3 Summary

The above two examples serve as an illustration of recursive Prolog programming. It is, however, true to say that the majority of Prolog programs of any reasonable size are likely to involve recursion. Indeed, recursion is the major control feature of most Prolog programs.

There are a few important points to remember when developing recursive programs. These are summarised below.

All recursive rules must have a stopping condition. This is important - if there is no stopping condition the rule will recurse forever.

In general, the stopping condition should appear above the recursive rule in the knowledge base. Again, this point is important. If the stopping condition is never found, this will also lead to infinite recursion.

In general, you must try and think in recursive terms when you are developing your Prolog programs. This will involve asking yourself such questions as:

How can I express this problem in terms of itself?

What is the stopping condition?

The resultant recursive rule will probably be of the general form :

```
recursive_rule_stop.
```

```
recursive_rule:- some_preliminary_computations,
                 recursive_rule,
                 some_final_computations.
```

6.3 The cut

Although backtracking is one of the most powerful features of the Prolog language, it is sometimes the case that we wish to control the amount of backtracking which takes place. This may be true for several different reasons, such as:

> we may not wish Prolog to tell us all of the possible solutions to a problem; indeed some of these solutions maybe of no use at all to us

> it may be the case that once a particular solution has been found it is unnecessary to find any more solutions; indeed further solutions may actually be incorrect

> large amounts of backtracking can make a program run very inefficiently, for two reasons. Firstly, a lot of backtracking can take some time to achieve; secondly, the markers which Prolog leaves during backtracking can use up quite a large amount of computer memory.

Prolog provides the user with a mechanism for controlling the level of backtracking that will take place within a particular program. This mechanism is known as the "cut".

The cut is denoted by an exclamation mark (!). When placed in a conjunction of goals the effect of the cut can be thought of as that of a one-way door which allows you to pass through it when travelling from left to right, but will then not allow you to go back through it from right to left. The cut goal always succeeds and cannot be resatisfied. For instance, consider the hypothetical rule example1 shown below:

```
example1 :- a,b,c,!,d,e,f.
```

As we know, Prolog will attempt to satisfy the example1 goal by satisfying the conjunction of goals to the right of the :- symbol, working through the goals from left (goal a) to right (goal f). If Prolog fails to satisfy a goal in the chain, it will backtrack in an attempt to resatisfy one of the previous goals. The cut has the effect of preventing backtracking once the ! symbol has been passed. What this means is that Prolog can backtrack as much as it wishes between the goals a, b and c but once goal c has been satisfied it will pass the ! symbol and the cut goal will succeed. Prolog will then continue along the chain of goals in an attempt to satisfy goals d, e and f. Indeed, it can backtrack amongst d, e and f if it should need to. At no point, however, can it backtrack past the ! symbol, even if this means that the whole of the example1 goal results in failure.

The cut is one of the most important concepts in Prolog. The placing of a cut within a particular program can make all the difference between a program which generates correct solutions and a program which generates long lists of solutions, some of which may be incorrect (or not required). Determining the correct place to position a cut in a program is, unfortunately, sometimes a difficult task. The following sections of this chapter give examples of the use of the cut which should help to illustrate its operation.

6.3.1 Ensuring the correct choice of rule

It is often the case that more than one form of a predicate is provided within a given program. This is particularly true in the case of recursive predicates (as we have seen in the previous section) where there are usually at least two distinct forms of the predicate, namely the recursive rule and the stopping condition. When developing such predicates it is necessary to ensure that Prolog will always choose the correct form of the predicate and will not, for instance, choose to use the recursive rule when it should be using the stopping condition. This type of situation can result in infinite recursion as discussed in Section 6.2.3. For example, consider the following predicate power(X,Y,Z) which succeeds provided that Z is X raised to the power of Y , that is:

$$Z = X^Y$$

The predicate is written

```
power(_,0,1). /* stopping condition */

power(X,Y,Z) :- L is Y - 1,
           power(X,L,M), /* recursive rule */
        Z is M * X.
```

If we were to give Prolog the following query

```
?- power(2,3,Z)./* calculate 2³*/
```

it will initially find a match with the recursive rule; X will be instantiated to 2, Y will be instantiated to 3 and the variable Z in the query will match (and hence share with) the variable Z in the rule. The subgoal

```
L is Y - 1
```

will result in L being instantiated to 2 (the result of the calculation 3 - 1). Prolog will then try to satisfy the subgoal

```
power(2,2,M).
```

This will result in Prolog reentering the knowledge base and encountering a match with (once again) the recursive rule. This recursive process will then continue in the manner depicted in Figure 6.1.

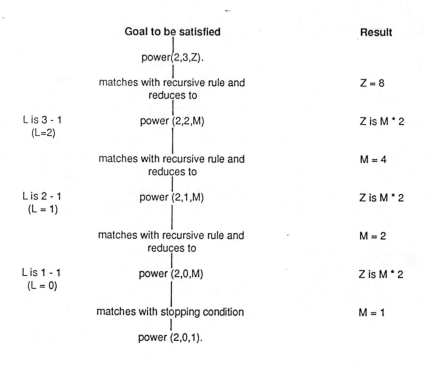

Fig. 6.1

The manner in which the predicate is operating is as below

$$2^3 = 2^2 * 2$$ recursive rule
but $$2^2 = 2^1 * 2$$ recursive rule
but $$2^2 = 2^0 * 2$$ recursive rule
but $$2^0 = 1$$ stopping condition

or, in more general terms,
$$X^Y = X^{Y-1} * X$$

but $X^{Y-1} = X^{Y-2} * X$
but $X^{Y-2} = X^{Y-3} * X$

.

.

etc....until
but $X^0 = 1$.

In other words, Prolog recurses until it has reduced the power to which the number is to be raised to zero. It then satisfies the stopping condition; the whole process terminates and the final result is displayed.

Consider, however, the consequence of asking Prolog to backtrack when it has given us the answer i.e. if we follow the response with a ; as below).

```
?- power(2,3,Z).
Z = 8 ? ;
```

What will happen in this case is that Prolog will go back and reconsider the last choice that it made. That choice was, of course, to use the stopping condition to match with the goal

```
power(2,0,M).
```

In reconsidering this choice Prolog is attempting to find another fact or rule in the knowledge base which will match with the above goal. That is, it is searching for another version of the power predicate. The only other version of the power predicate which exists in the knowledge base is, of course, the recursive rule

```
power(X,Y,Z):- L is Y - 1,
               power(X,L,M),
               Z is M * X.
```

This rule is, indeed, a correct match for the goal in question. Prolog would, therefore, make this match, resulting in X being instantiated to 2, Y being instantiated to 0, and Z sharing with M. Prolog would then proceed to calculate L to be -1 (0-1), and attempt to satisfy the goal

```
power(2,-1,M)
```

which is equivalent to trying to compute 2^{-1} . This, in turn would result in attempts to compute 2^{-2}, 2^{-3}, 2^{-4} etc. What is happening is infinite recursion (that is, the recursive goal is continually recreating itself and the stopping condition will never be found).
The above situation is obviously not desirable and can be avoided by placing a cut in the stopping condition and thus producing the new, more robust and reliable version of the power predicate which is given below:

```
power(_,0,1):- !.

power(X,Y,Z):- L is Y -1,
               power(X,L,M),
               Z is M * X.
```

The cut symbol is simply stating " if you have chosen this rule you must have made the correct choice and you can never backtrack and choose another rule in its place". This will, therefore, result in the (much more desirable) situation as illustrated below

```
?- power(2,3,Z).
Z = 8 ?;
no
```

You may have realised by now that the two recursive rules that were covered in the previous section of this chapter, could also produce similar, equally undesirable, results. This can easily be prevented by incorporating cuts in their respective stopping conditions as shown in the following versions of the programs.

```
/* factorial program */

factorial(1,1) :- !.

factorial(Number,Fact) :- Numb1 is Number - 1,
                          factorial(Numb1,Fact1),
                          Fact is Number * Fact1.

/* Fibonacci sequence */

fib(1,1) :- !.
fib(2,1) :- !.

fib(Number,Term) :- Numb1 is Number - 1,
                    Numb2 is Number - 2,
                    fib(Numb1,Term1),
                    fib(Numb2,Term2),
                    Term is Term1 + Term2.
```

In general, then, it is true to say that it is necessary to incorporate a cut into the stopping condition of a recursive predicate if it is possible for the recursive rule to be used in place of the stopping condition.

6.3.2 The cut-fail combination

Another common use of the cut is in conjunction with the fail predicate. The fail predicate is a standard predicate which will always fail, and hence cause backtracking. The cut can be placed in front of fail to prevent backtracking after the failure.

Consider the following program.

```
/* program to calculate candidates for
   voluntary redundancy */
```

```
redundancy(Employee)  :- service(Employee,Years),
                         Years > 20,
                         eligible(Employee).
```

/* an employee is a candidate for redundancy if
   he has more than 20 years service and he is
   eligible on general grounds */

```
eligible(Employee):- age(Employee,Years),
                     Years < 50,
                     !,fail.
```

/* an employee is not generally eligible for
   redundancy if he is less than 50 years old */

```
eligible(Employee):- manager(Employee),
                     !,fail.
```

/*a manager is not generally eligible for
redundancy*/

```
eligible(Employee):- shopfloor(Employee),
                     wage(Employee,Pay),
                     Pay < 15000,
                     Pay > 5000.
```

/* shopfloor workers are generally eligible
   for redundancy if they earn between £5000
   and £15000 */

/* a series of facts concerning years of service,
   status, age and wages of employees would also
   be required to complete this program */

Here the cut-fail combination is used to ensure that if an employee satisfies certain criteria which will render him ineligible he will not even be considered for eligibility under any other criteria. For instance, if an employee is less than 50 years old the fail predicate will cause the eligible goal to fail and the ! will ensure that the employee is not considered for eligibility under either of the other two eligible rules. Similarly, if an employee is a manager he cannot be considered to be eligible under the final eligible rule. Thus only employees who are 50 or older and are not managers will be considered for eligibility under the final eligible rule.

It should be noted that the cut-fail combination can generally be replaced by the use of the "not" predicate, which is another standard predicate. The goal not(X) will succeed if the goal X fails. The program above could thus be rewritten

```
redundancy(Employee):- service(Employee,Years),
                       Years > 20,
                       eligible(Employee).

eligible(Employee):- age(Employee,Years),
                     not(Years > 50),
                     not(manager(Employee)),
                     shop_floor(Employee),
                     wage(Employee,Pay),
                     Pay < 15000,
                     Pay > 5000.
```

Here the three eligible rules have been combined into one single rule. It is a debatable point as to which of the two versions of the program is more readable, and probably depends upon how well (or otherwise) you understand the cut. (It should also be mentioned that the goal not (Years < 50) could also be rewritten in the form Years >= 50 .)

6.4 Exercises

1. Type in the factorial program described in Sections 6.2.1. and 6.3.1. Place spy points on your program and run it to calculate 5!. Work through the output produced by the debugger and make sure that you can follow the recursive calls made by Prolog.

2. Develop a predicate sum(Int,Result) which succeeds if Result is the sum of all the integers between 0 and Int.

3. Develop a predicate average(Int,Result) which succeeds if Result is the average of the integers between 0 and Int. (Think about your answer to Exercise 2 above).

4. Develop a predicate sum(X,Y,Result) which succeeds if Result is the sum of all the integers between X and Y. (Think about your answer to 2 above again.)

5. Develop a predicate count(Z,No) which succeeds if No is the number of digits in the integer Z.

6. The Legendre polynomials of a real number y are defined recursively as below:

$$P_0(y) = 1$$

$$P_1(y) = y$$

$$P_n(y) = ((2n-1)yP_{n-1}(y) - (n-1)P_{n-2}(y))/n \text{ for } n > 1$$

Write a Prolog predicate pol(N,Y,P) which will compute P, the Nth polynomial of the real number Y.

6.5 Notes for Turbo Prolog programmers

6.5.1 Arithmetic

Turbo Prolog possesses much more powerful mathematical facilities than those provided by the majority of versions of the language. Turbo Prolog provides both integer and real arithmetic and its arithmetic capabilities are, therefore, similar to those described in the main body of this chapter.

It is the wide range of mathematical functions provided by the language, however, which make it much more suitable for the development of software which is highly mathematical in content. The most useful of these functions are listed in the following table (for a full list consult your Turbo Prolog manual).

Predicate	Explanation
abs(X)	absolute value of X
cos(X)	cosine of X
sin(X)	sine of X
tan(X)	tangent of X
exp(X)	e raised to the power of X
ln(X)	natural logarithm of X
log(X)	logarithm to base 10 of X
sqrt(X)	square root of X
mod	remainder after integer division
div	integer division

One other point which should be noted is the way in which Turbo Prolog performs calculations. The is operator does not exist in Turbo Prolog and calculations must be performed by means of the equals (=) sign; i.e. if, in a goal of the form

```
Variable = expression,
```

the Variable is uninstantiated the result will be that the goal will succeed, and the Variable will be instantiated to the value of the expression. If, however, the Variable is instantiated, success or failure of the goal will depend upon whether or not the value of the Variable is the same as that of the expression.

The terminal session below illustrates the operation of =.

```
Goal: X = 5/4.
X=1.25
1 Solution
Goal: 5/4 = Y.
Y=1.25
```

```
1 Solution
Goal: 5 = 6.
False
Goal: 6 = 6.
True
```

Chapter 7

Useful Structures

7.1 Lists

So far we have dealt solely with simple forms of data in our Prolog programs. These data have taken the form of objects such as fred, car, clock and locomotive and integers such as 9, 55 and 232. Such data are single items and have no structure to them. However, it is often desirable (and sometimes necessary) to structure data into collections of objects and/or integers known as lists.

The list is the basic data structure upon which many 'real- life' Prolog programs are based. A list is simply a collection of elements each of which can be an object or an integer. Prolog uses the simple terminology of denoting a list by enclosing the elements of the list in square brackets. The elements of the list are separated by commas. For example, the list which contains the elements fred, jack, susan and tom is written

[fred,jack,susan,tom]

and the list which contains the integers 1, 5, 68 is written

[1,5,68]

A list which contains no elements is called the empty list and is denoted

[]

A list is said to consist of two parts: a head and a tail. The head of the list is the first element of the list and the tail of the list is the list consisting of the remaining elements of the list (excluding the head). For instance, consider the list

[apple,pear,orange,grape].

The head of the above list is apple and the tail of the list

[pear,orange,grape].

The concept of 'head' and 'tail' is fundamental to the understanding of list manipulation in Prolog. It is important to remember that the head of a list is an element while the tail of a list is, itself, a list.

A list is, as you might have noticed, a recursive data structure because it consists of a head and another list (the tail). As with all recursive structures, it can be defined by a recursive definition.

One suitable recursive definition for a list is:

A list is a structure which contains two components, these being a head and a tail. The head of the list is the first element of the list and the tail of the list is the list which contains the remaining elements of the list.

The above definition can be illustrated by the following example.

Consider the list [a,b,c,d].

This list has head = a and tail = [b,c,d].

But the tail is also a list with head = b and tail = [c,d].

But the tail is also a list with head = c and tail = [d].

But the tail is also a list with head = d and tail = [].

The list [] is, of course, the empty list and our recursion ends here. As you will see in future examples, many forms of list manipulation involve using recursion until you get down to the empty list at which point you can recurse no further. i.e. this is the stopping condition because at this point you cannot break the empty list down any further into a head and a tail.

In general, the list with head H and tail T is denoted

    [H|T]

in Prolog, where the vertical bar symbol (|) is used to separate the head and the tail of the list. For instance, if a knowledge base contained the fact

    colours([red,orange,yellow,green,blue,indigo,violet])

and we asked the query

    ?- colours([H|T]).

the response obtained would be
    H = red
    T = [orange,yellow,green,blue,indigo,violet]?

7.2 Structures

As well as allowing us to group our data in the form of lists, Prolog also provides a means for creating structure within our predicates. This is achieved by giving structure to the arguments of a predicate by allowing them to have arguments themselves. In this way the factual information which is held within a predicate can be structured to reflect the structure of the actual real-world data which it is representing. For instance, consider the simple fact

> Jean has red hair.

This fact could, of course, be expressed in Prolog as

```
has(jean,red_hair).
```

There might also be a series of facts about people and the colour of their hair, eyes and other attributes of their appearance. The knowledge base might be something like:

```
has(mary,brown_hair).
has(tony,blue_eyes).
has(peter,black_beard).
has(tom,black_hair).
has(peter,brown_eyes).
etc............
```

Now if we wished to ask the hair colour of everyone in the knowledge base we would have to pose a query such as

```
?- has(X,Y).
```

and continually ask Prolog to backtrack by responding to the ? prompt with a ;. This would result in the response

```
X = jean
Y = red_hair? ;
X = mary
Y = brown_hair? ;
X = tony
Y = blue_eyes? ;
X = peter
Y = black_beard? ;
X = tom
Y = black_hair? ;
X = peter
Y = brown_eyes? ;
etc............
```

As you can see, this has resulted in a large amount of unnecessary information being output. This is because the data was not structured in such a manner so as to allow a more explicit query. One, much more useful, way of expressing exactly the same factual information would be as shown below:

```
has(jean,hair(red)).
has(mary,hair(brown)).
has(tony,eyes(blue)).
has(peter,beard(black)).
has(tom,hair(black)).
has(peter,eyes(brown)).
etc..............
```

Now, in order to ask the hair colour of everyone in the knowledge base we would simply pose the query

```
?- has(X,hair(Y)).
```

and again ask Prolog to backtrack after each solution. The resultant response would be

```
X = jean
Y = red? ;
X = mary
Y = brown? ;
X = tom
Y = black? ;
etc........
```

which is exactly the information which was required - no more, no less. Similarly we could ask the colour of Peter's beard

```
?- has(peter,beard(X)).
```

and receive the response

```
X = black?
```

It is, therefore, clearly important to think about the way that you are structuring your predicates and, in particular, the way in which they will be used when you wish to extract information from the knowledge base.

7.3 List manipulation

In order to develop programs which use information contained in the form of a list it is necessary to write rules which perform certain standard operations on lists. In general, when developing rules to manipulate lists it may be helpful to remember the following properties of a list.

A list is a recursive structure consisting of a head and a tail. The tail is, in turn, a list (this is where the recursion comes in).

It follows, therefore, that any rule to perform operations on a list is likely to be itself recursive. This is, in fact, the case and such a rule usually operates by performing the necessary manipulation on the head of the list and then using itself recursively to manipulate the tail of the list. Thus, such rules are often of the following format:

```
manipulate(list with head H and tail T):-
            perform manipulation on head H,
            recursively manipulate tail T.
```

or, in more Prolog-like terminology:

```
manipulate([H|T]):- process(H),
                    manipulate(T).
```

In addition to the above, it is also necessary to include a stopping condition which will halt the recursion when the entire list has been manipulated. If you consider the operation of the above rule, you will see what will, in fact, happen is that the list which remains to be manipulated will be continually reduced (by continually removing the head of the list). It follows, therefore, that the entire list will have been manipulated when the list has been reduced to the empty list. The full rule is thus of the form:

```
manipulate([]).
manipulate([H|T]):- process(H),
                    manipulate(T).
```

The above rule is phrased in such general terms that it may be somewhat difficult to follow on first reading. Also, in common with many attempts to generalise, the above form will apply in many situations - there will, however, be many other situations where another form of rule will be more applicable. The general concept of recursive list manipulation should become clearer after considering the development of Prolog predicates to perform some common operations on lists. The remainder of this section is devoted to a study of four such predicates.

7.3.1 Membership of a list

It is frequently necessary to determine whether or not a particular object is a member of a list. For instance, we might have a list X which contains the names of all the public houses in a particular town:

```
[black_bull,dun_cow,red_lion,kings_head,prospect].
```

Supposing we wish to ask Prolog whether or not there is a public house called The Red Lion in the town. What we are really asking is whether or not the object red_lion is a member of the list X; i.e. we would ask Prolog a query of the form:

```
?- member(red_lion,X).
```

In order to do this it would be necessary to define a predicate member(X,Y) which succeeds if the object X is a member of the list Y. It is important to note that X is an object (a single element) and Y is a list (a collection of elements) as this affects the operations which we are able to perform on these two arguments. One way of defining the member predicate is by exploiting the fact that a list is made up of two components - a head and a tail. This list property can be used in the following manner:

> The element X is a member of the list Y if X is the same as the head of the list Y. (Rule 1).

If the above is true, Prolog need look no further - it has proved that the element X is indeed a member of the list Y. If, however, this is not the case the following recursive rule must be used:

> The element X is a member of the list Y if X is a member of the tail of the list Y. (Rule 2).

This second rule is recursive because it uses member itself to prove whether or not the element X is a member of the tail of the list Y. The above two rules can be written in the conventional Prolog form as below:

```
member(X,[X|_]). /* Rule 1 */

member(X,[_|T]):- member(X,T). /* Rule 2 */
```

Notice that Rule 1 could have also been written

```
member(X,[H|_]):- X = H.
```

Notice also the use of the blank variable (_). In Rule 1, the blank variable is simply saying "we are testing to see if X is the same as the head of the list - we don't care what the tail is". In Rule 2 it is saying "we are testing to see if X is a member of the tail of the list - we don't care what the head is".

The way in which the member predicate operates is best demonstrated by an example. Consider the following query.

```
?- member(c,[a,b,c,d]).
```

The way in which Prolog proceeds in its search to answer this query is as set out below:

Enter knowledge base - try Rule 1 - this will fail because c is not the same as a (the head of the list).
Proceed to try Rule 2 - the initial goal (i.e. the query) will match with the head of the rule and X will be instantiated to c and T to [b,c,d]. The problem is thus reduced to that of satisfying the subgoal member(c,[b,c,d]).

Re-enter knowledge base - try Rule 1 - this will fail because c is not the same as b (the head of the list).
Proceed to try Rule 2 - the subgoal will match with the head of the rule and X will be instantiated to c and T to [c,d]. The problem is thus reduced to that of satisfying the subgoal member(c,[c,d]).

Re-enter knowledge base - try Rule 1 - this will succeed because c is the same as c (the head of the list).

Prolog will thus record a success and respond yes.

The above example demonstrates how Prolog proves that a particular object is a member of a list. But what if the object is not a member of the list? Where is the stopping condition to halt the procedure? Will Prolog continue to search for ever?

If the element being searched for is not a member of the list the problem will eventually reduce to that of attempting to satisfy the subgoal member(object,[]). Prolog will re-enter the knowledge base to try and prove or disprove this. It will first encounter Rule 1 which will fail because it is impossible to reduce the empty list [] to a head and a tail. Rule 2 will also fail for the same reason. Prolog will find no other rules which could be used to satisfy the subgoal and it will, therefore, respond no .

To summarise, the member predicate works in the following manner:

Prolog will continually remove elements from the head of the list until

either

the object being searched for is at the head of the current list - Rule 1 succeeds and Prolog replies yes

or

the list is reduced to the empty list and cannot, therefore, be reduced any further. Both rules fail and Prolog replies no.

The member predicate is an extremely important and useful piece of Prolog code which can be used as a building block for many other predicates which involve the manipulation of lists.

7.3.2 Appending two lists

It is often necessary to join (append) two lists together to form another list. This process is also known as concatenation. In order to perform this operation it is necessary to define a predicate append(X,Y,Z) which succeeds if Z is the list formed by appending the list Y to the end of the list X. For instance, the query

```
?- append([f,x,a],[e,g,i,l],M).
```

provokes the response

```
M = [f,x,a,e,g,i,l]?
```

The append rule works according to the following principle:

Consider the list with head H and tail T depicted in Figure 7.1 below:

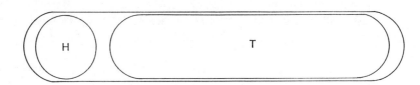

Fig. 7.1

The above list is to be appended to the list M in Figure 7.2 below:

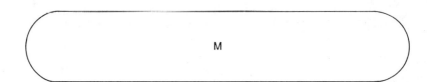

Fig. 7.2

The append process can be performed by placing H at the front (head) of the new list and appending T (the tail of the first list) to M (the second list) to form the tail T1 of the new list N as depicted in Figure 7.3 below:

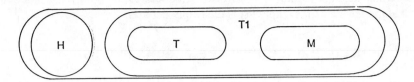

Fig. 7.3

This recursive process is written in Prolog as

```
append([H|T],M,[H|T1]):- append(T,M,T1).
```

The above rule also requires a stopping condition. In order to devise the stopping condition, it is necessary to consider exactly how the recursion in the append rule operates.

The append rule works by reducing the first argument to a head H and a tail T, placing H at the front of the new list and appending T to the second argument to form the tail of the new list. This append process is recursive and uses append itself. It will, therefore, involve reducing T to a head and a tail in a similar manner. This process will continue until the first argument of the recursively called append rule is [], the empty list. The stopping condition will thus take the form:

```
append([],L,L).
```

which simply states that the result of appending the empty list to any list L is the list L itself. The full version of append is thus:

```
append([],L,L).
append([H|T],M,[H|T1]):- append(T,M,T1).
```

7.3.3 Reversing a list

It is often desirable to reverse the contents of a list. This is done by defining a predicate reverse(X,Y) which succeeds if Y is the list formed by reversing the order of the elements in list X. The reverse predicate is most easily defined by using the append predicate developed in the previous section, and takes the form

```
reverse([],[]).
reverse([H|T],L):- reverse(T,M),
append(M,[H],L).
```

The above rule is based on the idea that you can reverse a list by appending a list containing its head ([H]) to the reverse of its tail (M). The stopping condition is reached when the first argument of reverse is reduced to the empty list and simply states that the reverse of the empty list is the empty list itself.

7.3.4 Counting the number of elements in a list

In order to count the number of elements in a list it is necessary to recursively count the number of elements in the tail of the list and then increment this number by one (i.e. the number of elements in a list is equal to the number of elements in the tail, plus one). The count predicate may be defined as count(X,Y) where Y is the number of elements in the list X.

The predicate takes the form

```
count([],0).
count([H|T],Y):- count(T,X),
                 Y is X + 1.
```

7.4 Exercises

1. Lists can be used to represent mathematical sets, where a set is simply a collection of elements. Develop predicates to perform the following common set operations

(a) **subset**. Define a predicate subset(X,Y) which succeeds if X is a subset of Y (i.e. all of the elements of the set X are contained within the set Y).

(b) **union**. Define a predicate union(X,Y,Z) which succeeds if Z is the union of the sets X and Y (i.e. Z is a set which contains all of the elements of X and Y).

(c) **intersection**. Define a predicate intersection(X,Y,Z) which succeeds if Z is the intersection of the two sets X and Y (i.e. Z contains those elements which are members of both X and Y).

2. (a) Implement a recursive predicate integers(Low,High,X) which succeeds if X is the list of integers between the limits Low and High. For example, the query

```
?- integers(2,10,X).
```

would produce the response

```
X = [2,3,4,5,6,7,8,9,10]?
```

(b) Implement the recursive predicate remove(X,Y,Z) which removes all of the multiples of the integer X from the list Y to produce a new list Z. For example, the query

98

```
?- remove(2,[3,4,5,6,7,8,9,10],Z).
```

would produce the response

```
Z = [3,5,7,9] ?
```

(c) Use the two predicates which you have developed in (a) and (b) above in a program to generate all the prime numbers from 2 to Limit inclusive, according to the following method:

1. Start with a list of all the integers between 2 and Limit.
2. Remove the smallest number from the list.
3. Include this number as a prime number.
4. Remove all multiples of this number from the list.
5. Repeat steps 2 to 5 until the list is empty.

7.5 Notes for Turbo Prolog programmers

The way in which Turbo Prolog deals with lists is identical to that described in the main body of this chapter. There are, however, differences in the manner in which Turbo Prolog allows the user to declare structures (as described in Section 7.2). Such structures are termed compound objects in Turbo Prolog.

7.5.1 Declaring compound objects

Consider the compound objects in the example given in Section 7.2. These would correspond to the following (identical) Turbo Prolog clauses:

```
clauses
has(jean,hair(red)).
has(mary,hair(brown)).
has(tony,eyes(blue)).
has(peter,beard(black)).
has(tom,hair(black)).
has(peter,eyes(brown)).
```

In order to use such clauses within a Turbo Prolog program it is necessary to declare the form of the compound objects within the domains declaration section. This would be done in the following manner:

```
domains
attributes = hair(colour) ; eyes(colour) ;
beard(colour)
name, colour = symbol
predicates
has(name,attributes)
```

99

Chapter 8

Built-In Predicates

8.1 The need for built-in predicates

So far this book has concentrated on how to design your own Prolog predicates. It would, however, be useful if predicates for common operations were provided by Prolog itself. Indeed, it would be silly if this were not the case, as this would mean that every Prolog programmer would have to write such predicates. This would result in a situation where common predicates would be written time and time again by different people - which would surely be a great waste of everyone's time.

For this reason Prolog provides the user with a number of built-in (or system) predicates. These can be used by the Prolog programmer as he would use any other predicates which he has defined himself. This chapter is devoted to coverage of such predicates. The more important built-in predicates are explained in detail while those which are less likely to be used by a beginner are covered briefly for reference purposes.

8.2 Input and Output

So far all of the Prolog programs developed in this book have used the standard Prolog 'query and response' interface. These programs have, as a result, been, to say the least, not very user-friendly and have required a knowledge of Prolog and its syntax in order for a user to run them. That is, anybody who wished to make use of any of the programs encountered so far in this book would need to know the following:

which predicates are available in the program, the purpose of each of them and the number and form of the arguments of these predicates

sufficient knowledge of Prolog to be able to phrase his queries in an acceptable form

sufficient knowledge of Prolog to be able to interpret the rather stark X = or yes/no answers which Prolog provides as response.

This is obviously not an ideal set of circumstances. Ideally any program which you produce should be designed to be interactive and as user-friendly as possible. An interactive program is one which acts in a conversational mode with the user. In other words, running the program is like having a question and answer session with the computer. A user-friendly program is one which can be used by a person who is not experienced in the use of computers. Such a program should be able to be used with a minimal amount of prior training. It is particularly important that expert systems software should be both interactive and user- friendly because it is often designed to be used as a consultative tool by non-computer-literate people. The next chapter of this book covers the topic of user-interface design in more detail. However, there are a number of basic concepts regarding input and output in Prolog programs which are worthy of mention here.

As stated above, user-friendly software should be designed so that it can be readily usable by people whose knowledge and experience of computers may be quite limited. This means that programs:

> should be as self-explanatory as possible

> should provide answers to (or ask questions of) the user in terminology which he will find easy to understand

> should allow the user to ask questions (or provide answers) in as English-like a fashion as possible.

Prolog provides a number of built-in predicates to help the programmer to construct such user-friendly software. The remainder of this section is devoted to the coverage of these predicates.The operation of each of the predicates is described briefly followed by example programs to illustrate their use.

8.2.1 Writing information to the screen

Prolog provides the write predicate for writing information to the screen. The goal write(X) causes Prolog to write the value of the term X to the screen. The term X may be an object, integer or a variable. For instance, if X is an instantiated variable and has the value peter execution of the goal write(X) will cause your computer to display

```
peter
```

on the screen. If X is, however, an uninstantiated variable, this will be indicated by writing a variable number (such as _53) to the screen. As with all of the built-in predicates for input and output, the write predicate can only succeed once and cannot be resatisfied.

8.2.2 Formatting output

There are two built-in predicates which are used in conjunction with the write predicate to produce more professionally formatted output. The first of these is the tab predicate.

The goal tab(X) causes X blanks to be output to the screen. This means that X should be instantiated to an integer. For example, the goal tab(5) will cause five blanks to be output to the screen so that the next piece of information to be written to the screen will appear five spaces to the right of that which was previously displayed.

The second of these predicates is the nl predicate. The abbreviation nl stands for newline and the nl goal causes the next piece of information to be displayed on the next line of the screen.

For instance, the segment of code

```
write(this),tab(1),write(is),tab(2),write(a),tab(3),
write(message),nl,write(so),write(is),write(this).
```

would cause the message

```
this is a   message
soisthis
```

to be output.

8.2.3 Writing lists

In order to create interactive software it is necessary to be able to cause your programs to print out messages to the user. One way of doing this is by storing the messages within your program in the form of lists of objects where each of the objects is a word in a sentence and the whole list represents an entire sentence. For instance, the message

```
What is your name?
```

could be stored as the list

```
['What',is,your,'name?']
```

Notice that the objects 'What' and 'name' must be enclosed in single quotes. This is because they contain characters which are not normally allowed as part of an object (i.e. they are not lower case).

In order to output such a list it is necessary to print it element by element with spaces between the elements. This can be achieved by using a rule such as write_list defined below:

```
write_list([]).
write_list([H|T]):- write(H),tab(1),write_list(T).
```

The write_list predicate operates by using the write predicate to write the head H of the

103

list. It then tabs one space and recursively uses itself to write the tail T of the list. The stopping condition is reached when an attempt is made to write_list the empty list.

Execution of the goal

```
write_list(['What',is,your,'name?']).
```

within a program would thus cause the text

```
What is your name?
```

to be output.

8.2.4 Reading information from the keyboard

The read predicate is used to read information from the keyboard. The goal read(X) causes Prolog to read a series of characters (i.e. a term) from the keyboard. The term must be terminated by a full stop (.) and followed by the return key. Prolog will prompt the user for input with the following prompt

```
| :
```

If the variable X is uninstantiated, the goal read(X) will result in X being instantiated to the term which has been input. If, however, the variable X is already instantiated, the goal read(X) will cause X to be compared with the term which has been read. If these two terms match, the goal read(X) will succeed, otherwise it will fail.

8.2.5 A sample interactive program

Consider the following program which is designed to act as an aid for the motorist who is considering purchasing a new car:

```
/* car selection program */

car_select:-
write_list(['Answer',the,following,questions]),
nl,nl,
write_list(['How',much,do,you,wish,to,'spend?']),
nl,read(Amount),
write_list(['Do',you,want,a,saloon,car,or,
an,estate,'car?']),nl,
read(Type),
write_list(['Do',you,want,a,british,',',
american,or,japanese,'car?']),nl,
read(Country),
```

```
find_car(Amount,Make,Type,Country,Cost),
write_list(['The',most,suitable,car,is,a]),
write(Make),tab(1),
write_list([which,costs]),write('£'),
write(Cost),nl.

find_car(Amount,Make,Type,Country,Cost):-
car(Make,Type,Country,Cost),
Cost =< Amount.

car('Toysun',saloon,japanese,4000).
car('Toysun',estate,japanese,4500).
car('Ford',saloon,american,4000).
car('Ford',estate,american,4500).
car('Roller',saloon,british,50000).
car('Uaston',saloon,british,4500).
car('Uaston',estate,british,5000).

write_list([]).
write_list([H|T]):- write(H),tab(1),write_list(T).
```

The terminal session below illustrates the operation of this program:

```
?- ['car.pl'].
car.pl consulted
yes

?- car_select.
Answer the following questions

How much do you wish to spend?
|: 4000.
Do you want a saloon car or an estate car?
|: saloon.
Do you want a british, american or japanese car?
|: american.
The most suitable car is a Ford which costs £4000
yes

?- car_select.
Answer the following questions

How much do you wish to spend?
|: 3000.
Do you want a saloon car or an estate car?
|: saloon.
```

```
Do you want a british, american or japanese car?
|: japanese.
no

?- car_select.
Answer the following questions

How much do you wish to spend?
|: 40000.
Do you want a saloon car or an estate car?
|: saloon.
Do you want a british, american or japanese car?
|: british.
The most suitable car is a Uaston which costs £4500
yes

?- car_select.
Answer the following questions

How much do you wish to spend?
|: 55000
Do you want a saloon car or an estate car?
|: saloon.
Do you want a british, american or japanese car?
|: british.
The most suitable car is a Roller which costs £50000
yes

?- car_select.
Answer the following questions

How much do you wish to spend?
|: 5000.
Do you want a saloon car or an estate car?
|: estate.
Do you want a british, american or japanese car?
|: american
The most suitable car is a Ford which costs £4500
yes
```

The above example is, obviously, simplified but you can easily imagine how the database of car facts could be extended to include many more different makes and model of car. Similarly, the questions which are asked of the user could also be extended to enable a much more specific car to be identified.

It could also be (quite rightly) said that the program is far from user-friendly. In particular, if it cannot find a car to match the user's requirements it simply replies with a rather unhelpful (and ill-mannered) no!

8.2.6 Reading and writing single characters

The input and output predicates which have been covered so far in this chapter are concerned with the input and output of entire terms, such as objects or, if you like, words and sentences. Prolog also provides predicates for the input and output of single characters. These predicates, which correspond in their operation to the predicates read and write, are get and put.

The get predicate is used to input a single character from the keyboard. The goal get(X) causes the uninstantiated variable X to be instantiated to an integer, which is the ASCII code of the next character to be input at the keyboard. ASCII (American Standard Code for Information Interchange) is a standard, internationally recognised, code which is used to store characters within computer memory. The entire code is contained in Appendix A.

If X is instantiated, the goal get(X) causes the ASCII code of the character which is input to be compared with the value of X. If these match the goal will succeed; otherwise it will fail.

It should be noted that get(X) can only be used for printing characters (i.e. those characters which can be displayed on the screen of your computer) and will skip any non-printing characters. There is, however, a predicate get0(X) which may be used to input any ASCII character (including non-printing characters).

The put predicate is used to write single characters to the screen. If the variable X is instantiated to an ASCII code the goal put(X) will cause the corresponding character to be written to the screen.

The following terminal session illustrates the operation of get and put:

```
?- get (X) .
| : z
X =122  yes

?- get (85) .
| : U
yes

?- get (114) .
| : a
no
```

```
?-
put(114),put(117),put(98),put(98),put(105),put(115),
put(104).
rubbishyes

?-
put(114),put(117),put(98),put(98),put(105),put(115),
put(104),nl.
rubbish
yes
```

The previous terminal session should be read in conjunction with Appendix A, the list of ASCII codes.

8.2.7 Writing strings

A "string" is a collection of characters contained in double quotes such as

```
"fred"   "abcde"   "I am a string!"
```

Prolog represents each of the characters within a string as an ASCII code and the entire string is represented as a list of ASCII codes. Hence, the three strings above would be stored by Prolog as:

```
[102,114,101,100]
[97,98,99,100,101]
[73,32,97,107,32,97,32,115,116,114,105,110,103,33].
```

It should be noted that strings must not be confused with groups of characters which are contained in single quotes such as

```
'Fred' '£5'   'Monte Carlo'
```

which are simple objects (see Section 4.5).

In order to write a string it is necessary to do so character by character - if you ask Prolog to write the entire string at once all that will be output will be the corresponding list of ASCII codes. For instance, the command

```
write("Type in a number")
```

within a Prolog program would result in the unreadable message

```
[84,121,112,101,32,105,110,32,97,32,110,117,109,98,1
01,114]
```

being output! In order to output the actual text of the string it is necessary to create a rule write_string(X) as below:

```
write_string([]).
write_string([H|T]):- put(H),write_string(T).
```

This rule operates by using put to print the head of the list of ASCII codes and then using write_string recursively to print the tail of the list. It is, of course, very similar in construction to the write_list predicate which was defined in Section 8.2.3.

This means that, instead of using the write_list predicate as in the program in Section 8.2.5, it is possible to phrase the messages within a program in the form of strings. Indeed, it should be noted that there are, in fact, three methods of causing a Prolog program to output a message such as

```
Type in your name
```

These are:

First, you can use write_list to output a list of objects, where each of the objects is a word within the message:

```
write_list(['Type',in,your,name]).
```

Second, you can use write_string to output a string:

```
write_string("Type in your name").
```

Third, you can use the write predicate to output an object, where the entire message is treated as a single object:

```
write('Type in your name').
```

8.2.8 The use of files

Sometimes it is desirable to store large amounts of data on a secondary storage device such as magnetic disc. This is particularly useful if, for instance,

> a program needs to read large amounts of data each time it is run. It would be wasteful to have to type all of the data in at the keyboard each time that you wished to run the program

> a permanent copy of some output data from a program is required.

In such circumstances it is common practice to store data in the form of a file. A file is basically a sequence of characters stored on an external storage device; which is nowadays usually a magnetic disc unit of some shape or form.

Prolog allows you to use files to store data in conjunction with the predicates read, write, get and put as described in the previous sections of this chapter. This is done by telling Prolog that the input is to come from (or go to) a file rather than the keyboard (or screen). The predicates described below are provided for this purpose.

tell - The goal tell(X) instructs Prolog that all output from the program produced by the predicates write, put, tab etc. will henceforth be sent to the file X. The term X must be a valid filename for the particular computer system under use. If the file X does not already exist execution of the goal tell(X) will cause a file of that name to be created. If the file X does already exist it will be overwritten (i.e. any data already contained within the file will be lost and replaced by the new data written by the program).

told - The goal told is used when the program has finished writing to the current output file. It causes the file to be closed and any further output will be directed to the computer screen (or printer).

telling - This predicate is used to discover the name of the file which is currently being written to. The goal telling(X) succeeds when X is instantiated to the name of the current output file.

see - The goal see(X) switches input to the file named X and is, in effect, the converse of the predicate tell described previously. Correspondingly, the predicate seen is used to close the input file and cause input to revert back to the keyboard. The goal seeing(X) is used to discover the name of the current input file.

It should be noted that the standard file user represents the keyboard for input and the screen for output.

The example program below will create a file example.dat containing the integers between 1 and 100, each integer being written on a new line.

```
file_store:- tell('example.dat'),
             write_numbers(1,100),
             told.

write_numbers(Upper,Upper):- write(Upper),nl.

write_numbers(Lower,Upper):- write(Lower),nl,
                             Lower1 is Lower + 1,
                             write_numbers(Lower1,Upper).
```

8.3 Self-modification of the knowledge base

The philosophy behind the concept of expert systems is that the system should be able to act as a consultant in some restricted area of human expertise. In order to be able to do so, the expert system must be able to model, as closely as possible the way in which a human expert deduces the answer to a particular problem. This means that the system should have the ability to learn from its experiences (and mistakes!). That is, the knowledge base should be dynamic (i.e. changing with time) and not static (fixed). Prolog provides the predicate assert for this purpose. It also provides a predicate retract which allows the system to unlearn (i.e. forget) that which has been previously asserted.

The assert predicate takes two forms; asserta and assertz. The goal asserta(X) causes the clause X to be added to the beginning of the current knowledge base, preceding any of the existing clauses. The goal assertz(X) operates in a similar manner, however in this case the clause X is placed at the end of the current knowledge base. (Note. Some versions of Prolog also provide a predicate assert which is identical in operation to assertz). The term X must be a valid Prolog clause; that is, a fact or a rule.

In this manner it is possible for the knowledge base to grow as the terminal session proceeds. For instance, the following program code illustrates how a series of facts can be incorporated within a knowledge base for later use.

```
initialise:- write('What is your name?'),nl,
             read(Name),
             assertz(user(Name)),
             write('Are you male or female?'),nl,
             read(Gender),
             add_gender_fact(Gender,Name).

add_gender_fact(male,Name):- assertz(male(Name)).

add_gender_fact(female,Name):-
assertz(female(Name)).
```

Running the initialise rule would result in a terminal session such as below.

```
?- initialise.
What is your name?
|: julie.
Are you male or female?
|: female.
yes
```

The knowledge base has now been initialised to include the facts that the user's name is Julie and that she is female. These facts can thus be used within later rules during the session. The current state of the knowledge base can be displayed by using the standard predicate listing. Simply typing the command

```
?- listing.
```

will result in all of the clauses within the knowledge base being displayed on the screen. You can also specify that you wish to display a particular clause, as below:

```
?- listing(female).
female(julie).
yes

?- listing(user).
user(julie).
yes

?- listing(male).
yes
```

It is, however, sometimes desirable to be able to remove facts and rules from the knowledge base. For instance, once the initialise rule described above has been run the facts about the user's name and gender will remain within the knowledge base throughout that terminal session. If we were to run initialise again, perhaps for a different user, it might first be sensible to remove the facts about the previous user. This can be done by using the predicate retract.

The retract predicate is used to remove facts and rules(i.e. clauses) from the knowledge base. The goal retract(X) causes the first clause of the form X to be removed from the current knowledge base. The terminal session below would remove the facts about Julie from the knowledge base:

```
?- retract(user(X)).
X = julie ?
yes

?- retract(female(X)).
X = julie ?
yes
```

8.4 Other built-in predicates

This section is designed to serve as a reference manual in that it provides brief coverage of the remaining built-in predicates which are provided by Prolog (i.e. if a predicate has been discussed in detail in an earlier section of the book it is not included in this section). The operation of each predicate is summarised followed by a simple example of its use. The predicates are listed in alphabetical order.

8.4.1 abolish

Deletes all clauses with a given name and arity (number of arguments). The goal abolish(X,Y) causes all clauses with predicate X and arity Y to be retracted from the knowledge base. For instance, if a knowledge base contains the two friends clauses

```
friends(peter,jane).
friends(tom,dick,harry).
```

the goal

```
?- abolish(friends,2).
```

will remove the first of the two clauses.

8.4.2 arg

Obtains the nth argument of a structure. The goal arg(N,X,Y) causes the variable Y to be matched with the Nth argument of the structure X. Note that, as demonstrated in the example below, a list is considered to be a structure of arity 2 (i.e. with two arguments - a head and a tail).

```
?- arg(2,[fred,jane,dick,peter],X).
X = [jane,dick,peter]?
yes

?- arg(3,fruit(apple,orange,pear),Y).
Y = pear?
yes
```

8.4.3 atom

This tests if a term is currently an atom (where atom is another name for a Prolog object). The goal atom(X) succeeds if X is an atom (i.e. an object).

```
?- atom(X).
no
?- atom(25).
no
?- atom(tower).
yes
?- atom('Hello there').
yes
```

8.4.4 atomic

This tests if a term is currently an atom (object) or an integer. The goal atomic(X) succeeds if X is either an integer or an atom.

```
?- atomic(fred).
yes

?-atomic(67).
yes

?-atomic(Variable).
no
```

8.4.5 call

The goal call(X) succeeds if the goal X succeeds. That is, for example, the goal call(male(X)) succeeds provided that the goal male(X) succeeds. This would appear to be a pointless exercise as the goal call(male(X)) could simply be replaced by the goal male(X). There are, however, instances where the name of the goal in question is not known at the time of writing the program, but will be computed at execution time (e.g. by using univ - see Section 8.4.19). In such cases there is no alternative but to use call(X).

8.4.6 clause

The goal clause(H,B) causes a search to take place within the knowledge base for a clause with head H and body B. For instance, if the knowledge base contains the clauses

```
member(X,[X|_]).
member(X,[_|Y]):- member(X,Y).
```

the following terminal session illustrates the operation of the predicate clause

```
?- clause(member(X,Y),L).

X = _1
Y = [_1|_2]
L = true ? ;

X = _3
Y = [_2|_4]
L = member(_3,_4) ? ;

no
```

8.4.7 consult/reconsult

The goal consult(X) is used to add the clauses within the file X to the current knowledge base. A shorthand form of consult(X) is [X].

114

The goal reconsult(X) is similar in operation apart from the fact that it causes the clauses within the file X to replace any clauses of the same name which already exist in the knowledge base. A shorthand form of reconsult(X) is [-X].

```
?- consult('file.pl').
file.pl consulted
yes

?- [-'file.pl'].
file.pl reconsulted
yes
```

8.4.8 display

The goal display(X) causes the term X to be displayed, ignoring any operator declarations (see Section 8.4.15).

```
?- display(5+4).
+(5,4).
yes

?- display(eats(tony,hamburger)).
eats(tony,hamburger).
yes
```

8.4.9 fail/true

The goal `fail` always fails and can thus be used to cause backtracking to take place. For example, the query

```
solve(X),write(X),nl,fail.
```

would cause all the possible solutions to the goal solve(X) to be written, each on a new line. The predicate fail is also used in conjunction with the cut (!).

The goal `true` is the converse of `fail` and always succeeds.

8.4.10 functor

The predicate functor has three arguments. The first represents a clause, the second its name (functor) and the third its arity (number of arguments).

```
?- functor(house(semi,1953,35000),X,Y).
X = house
Y = 3 ?
yes
```

8.4.11 integer

The goal integer(X) succeeds if the term X is an integer.

```
?- integer(56).
yes

?- integer(X).
no

?- integer(museum).
no
```

8.4.12 listing

Used to display the current clauses in the knowledge base. The goal listing(X) causes all of the clauses for predicate X to be displayed. The goal listing causes all of the clauses in the current knowledge base to be displayed.

8.4.13 name

Used to convert between a list of ASCII codes and an object consisting of their character equivalents. The goal name(X,Y) succeeds provided that the characters for the object X are given by the ASCII codes in the list Y.

```
?- name(telephone,X).
X = [116,101,108,101,112,104,111,110,101] ?
yes

?- name(X,[112,108,97,110,101]).
X = plane ?
yes
```

8.4.14 not

The goal not(X) succeeds if the goal X fails and vice versa, as shown on the next page.

```
?- assertz(tall(tree)).
yes

?- not(tall(tree)).
no

?- not(small(tree)).
yes
```

8.4.15 op

Used to declare an operator. The predicate op has three arguments. These are given below:

Precedence - an integer defining the operator's precedence

Associativity - an object defining the associative properties of the operator. This object must be one of the following:

fx fy	prefix operator
xfx xfy yfx	infix operator
xf yf	postfix operator

where f represents the operator and x and y represent arguments. y means the argument can contain operators of the same or lower precedence. x means that the argument can only contain operations of lower precedence.

Functor - the name of the operator

A list of the standard operators which are provided by Prolog is contained in Appendix B.

To define an operator the op predicate is used as below:

```
?- op(100,xfy,marries).
yes

?- [user].
| adrian marries pat.
| tony marries marie.
| simon marries natalie.
CTRL Z

?- X marries Y.
X = adrian
Y = pat? ;

X = tony
Y = marie? ;

X = simon
Y = natalie? ;
no
```

8.4.16 repeat

Used to generate an infinite sequence of goals. The predicate repeat is defined as

```
repeat.
repeat:- repeat.
```

and thus recurses infinitely. It is used to introduce a loop (iteration) within a program.

8.4.17 retractall

Similar to abolish. The goal retractall(X) causes all clauses whose "heads" match X to be removed from the current knowledge base.

8.4.18 skip

The goal skip(X) will cause input to skip ahead until the character X is read.

8.4.19 univ (=..)

The predicate =.. (pronounced univ) is used to create a structure from a list. X=..L can be taken to mean "L is the list consisting of the functor (name) of the clause X followed by the arguments of X".

```
?- X=..[furniture,chair,table,sofa].
X = furniture(chair,table,sofa)?
yes
```

8.4.20 var/nonvar

The goal var(X) succeeds if X is an uninstantiated variable. The predicate nonvar is the converse of var and the goal nonvar(X) succeeds if X is not an uninstantiated variable.

```
?- var(X).
yes

?- var(5).
no
?- nonvar(5).
yes

?- nonvar(X)
no
```

8.5 Exercises

1. Modify the car selection program in Section 8.2.5 so that it is more "user-friendly". In particular, change the program so that it informs the user

```
No suitable car can be found
```

when no match is found, rather than replying no.

2. Write a program which will input an integer value and output the number of digits in the square of that integer.

3. Write a program which will request the user for the following pieces of information:
today's date
the day of the week on which January 1st fell this year
The program should then proceed to compute which day of the week it is today.

4. Write a program which will produce a calendar for any year in the range 1975 to 1999.

8.6 Notes for Turbo Prolog programmers

There are a large number of differences between the built-in predicates which are provided by Turbo Prolog and those described in the main body of this chapter. It is the purpose of this section to explain these differences and to describe the operation of some of the large number of additional predicates which Turbo Prolog provides.

8.6.1 Input and Output

This section discusses the input/output facilities of Turbo Prolog.

8.6.1.1 Writing information to the screen

The operation of the write predicate is similar to that described in Section 8.2.1 in all but two respects:

the write predicate is allowed to have more than one argument in Turbo Prolog
in Turbo Prolog the write predicate can be used to write strings contained in double quotes (remember objects contained in single quotes are not allowed).

That is, the Prolog clauses

```
write('My name is '),write(Name)
```

would be rewritten

```
write("My name is ",Name)
```

in Turbo Prolog.

The operation of the nl predicate is exactly the same in Turbo Prolog. However, the characters \n can also be used within an output string to achieve a similar effect.

That is, the clauses

```
write("hello"),nl,write("there")
```

and

```
write("hello\nthere")
```

are equivalent in their operation.

Note. The predicates tab and get do not exist in Turbo Prolog.

8.6.1.2 Reading information from the keyboard

The predicates which are provided for reading information from the keyboard are quite different from those outlined in Section 8.2.4 and are listed below:

readln(Text) - reads a string (Text) from the keyboard. The string is terminated by pressing the return key.

readint(Int) - reads an integer value from the keyboard.

readreal(Real) - reads a real number value from the keyboard.

readchar(Char) - reads a single character from the keyboard.

8.6.2 Using files

The commands for using files are completely different from those described in Section 8.2.8. This is because Turbo Prolog provides much more extensive file processing facilities than most versions of Prolog. The major predicates provided for file handling are summarised below:

openread(Logicalname,Physicalname) - used to open a file for reading. Logicalname is the name by which the file will be referred to within the program, whereas Physicalname is the actual name of the file by which it was stored on disc.

`openwrite(Logicalname,Physicalname)` - similar to above but used to open a file for writing.

`closefile(Logicalname)` - used to close a file after it has been written to (or read from).

`readdevice(Logicalname)` - used to switch the current read device to that defined by Logicalname.

`writedevice(Logicalname)` - equivalent to above, but for writing.

For example, the program in Section 8.2.8 would be written as below:

```
domains
  file = example
  numb = integer
predicates
  file_store
  write_numbers(numb,numb)
clauses
  file_store:- openwrite(example,"b:temp"),
               writedevice(example),
               write_numbers(1,100),
               closefile(example),
               writedevice(screen),
               write("done\n").

  write_numbers(Upper,Upper):- write(Upper),nl.

  write_numbers(Lower,Upper):-
  write(Lower),nl,
  Lower1 = Lower + 1,
  write_numbers(Lower1,Upper).
```

Turbo Prolog provides many other predicates to facilitate file processing. These are covered in detail in the Turbo Prolog manual.

8.6.3 assert and retract

Turbo Prolog allows the use of assert and retract, but there are some differences in the operation and use of these predicates. These are:

they can only be used for adding or deleting facts (and not rules).

predicates which are to be asserted or retracted must be declared in a database declaration section.

The example below (which is based on the example in Section 8.3) illustrates the operation of these predicates:

```
domains
    name , response = symbol
    gender = male ; female
database
    user(name)
    male(name)
    female(name)
predicates
    initialise
    add_gender_fact(gender,name)
    find_gender(response,gender)
clauses
    initialise:- write("What is your name?\n"),
                 readln(Name),
                 assertz(user(Name)),
                 write("Are you male?\n"),
                 readln(Response),
                 find_gender(Response,Gender),
                 add_gender_fact(Gender,Name).

    add_gender_fact(male,Name):-
                 assertz(male(Name)).
    add_gender_fact(female,Name):-
                 assertz(female(Name)).

    find_gender(yes,male).
    find_gender(no,female).
```

8.6.4 Other built-in predicates

For reference purposes, this section compares those predicates listed in Section 8.4 with those provided by Turbo Prolog.

The following predicates do not exist in Turbo Prolog:

abolish, arg, atom, atomic, call, clause, reconsult, true, functor, integer, listing, name, op, repeat, retractall, skip, univ, var, nonvar

The following predicates exist and operate in a similar manner to that described in Section 8.4

consult, fail, not, display (used to display an object)

Turbo Prolog provides many other predicates, full explanations of which can be found in the Turbo Prolog manual. The following selected predicates may, however, be of interest to the beginner.

bound(X)/free(X) - these are somewhat similar to var and nonvar and are used in a program to determine whether or not a variable X is bound (instantiated) or free (uninstantiated)

date(Year,Month,Day) - used to read the date from the computer's internal clock

exit -halts execution of a program and returns the user to the Turbo Prolog menu system

time(Hours,Mins,Secs,Hundredths) - used to read the time from the computer's internal clock

Turbo Prolog also provides a large number of predicates for use in conjunction with its extensive screen and string handling facilities. Some of these are discussed in Section 9.4.

Chapter 9

User-Interface Design

9.1 Introduction

This section discusses the various considerations which are important in the design of a user interface. First, however, a word on the interface with which we have been dealing so far.

9.1.1 The standard Prolog interface

As mentioned in Chapter 8, the standard interface which Prolog presents to the user, is to say the least, not very user friendly. In order to obtain any useful information or knowledge from Prolog the user must first have some knowledge of how the language functions. He must be familiar with the concept of query mode and be able to phrase his questions in correct Prolog syntax. He must also know which predicates are available in the knowledge base for his use and which of those predicates in particular will produce the answer to his question.

This situation might be quite acceptable to Prolog programmers but is of no use at all to the naive user who wishes to make use of an expert system which has been produced in Prolog. Such a user may have no previous knowledge and experience of computers and computing terminology, let alone any knowledge about the intricacies and peculiarities of the Prolog language.

It is for this reason that it is often necessary to construct an intelligent user interface which will 'sit on top' of such a Prolog expert system. Such an interface will enable the user to communicate with the expert system in the sort of language with which he is familiar (ideally this will be English).

However, before going on to discuss the complexities of designing interfaces to deal with English-like dialogue it would be useful to consider the question of user-interface design in general.

9.1.2 Considerations in user-interface design

The field of user-interface design is one of the least understood areas of software engineering. Although it is generally recognised that any usable piece of software must have a good user interface, there are few well-tried methods available for the design and implementation of user-interfaces. This is probably because the field is so wide and varied; indeed it is as varied as the needs of users themselves.

When setting out to design a user-interface for any piece of software it is necessary to ask yourself such questions as :

Who exactly are the users that I am targetting my software at?

Do I have a single set of users or is the software going to be used by a number of different groups of users? (Presumably each of the different groups will have different needs and expectations).

These questions may, of course, already have been answered by the market research which should have been undertaken prior to taking the decision to produce the software. In any case, it would be a very foolish software designer who embarks upon the task of developing a large piece of software without first identifying who his target audience is.

Having decided who your users are it is necessary to design a user-interface which will be appropriate for their use. This stage will involve answering the following question :

What sort of interface is most appropriate for the system?

There are several forms of user-interface which could be chosen. These include :

a dialogue system

a menu-driven system

a graphical interface

an interface involving voice input

The first two of the above four user-interfaces are in common use in many current software systems.

A dialogue system is as the name suggests, a system in which the user takes part in an interactive conversation with the computer. The computer will produce certain prompts to which the user will have to respond. The example program in Section 8.2.5 utilises a simple dialogue.

Menu-driven systems are probably the most common type of interface currently available in commercial software. A menu- driven system comprises a series of choices in the form of a "menu". These choices are listed on the computer screen and the user is requested to choose one option from the range available. Many menu-driven systems actually comprise a hierarchy of many menus. In such a system the user is initially presented with a main menu whose options direct him towards other, more detailed, menus. After working through a succession of such menus the user will eventually reach the actual function which he requires.

The latter two of the previously listed user-interfaces are in less common use.

A graphical interface provides the user with a series of pictures or "icons", each of which has been designed to graphically represent some real world object. The user then chooses the particular icon which represents the function which he wishes to use. The method of choosing the icon may involve pointing to it with the cursor (which may perhaps be moved by means of a device such as a mouse), by the use of a touch sensitive screen, or by some other special controls. One good example of an extremely user friendly graphical interface is the now traditional arcade game, such as space invaders.

The concept of voice input is still relatively new and is a growth area of current A.I. research. There are very few systems which deal with such input and those which do so can recognise only a very restricted number of command words.

The choice as to which type of user-interface is most appropriate may also be, to some extent, determined by the hardware which is available for use. For instance, the following facilities may or may not be available for incorporation within your user-interface :

    graphics

    sound

    colour

    use of devices such as mouse, touch sensitive screen, etc.

Having decided upon the particular form of the user-interface and of the facilities and devices which are to be used there are a number of other important points which must be observed. these are :

    Design your text to be readable by your users.

    Don't use jargon.

    Don't be patronising - aim your dialogue at the correct level (i.e. not too high or too low)

    Try and make your system as enjoyable to use as possible

    Be careful with your use of colour and/or sound

The above points are, to a large extent, commonsense and are, of course, also extremely subjective. There has, however, recently been a considerable amount of research undertaken in the area of user-interface design in an attempt to determine the answer to questions such as :

Which colours should be used in a user-interface?

Which commands are most easily remembered?

Which type of interfaces are easier to learn to use, especially for the novice user?

One useful approach to user-interface design is that known as prototyping. Prototyping involves the production of samples of menus and dialogues at an early stage and allowing the user to experiment with them. This enables the user to familiarise himself with the format of the user interface and can thus lead to improvements in the interface. This process can be repeated several times in order to allow for further improvements. The process of prototyping thus involves continual interaction between the software designer and the user and should, therefore, result in a better understanding on either side as to what form the user interface should take.

Prototyping is particularly useful when the system is being designed for a user who has little or no experience of computers as it can help the user to get to know the system and, perhaps, decide what he really wants the system to do for him. This is much more effective than not involving the user at all during the design stage, which can result in the production of a piece of software which is totally unusable (and hence useless!).

To summarise, the design of a user-interface is a difficult process for which there are few, if any, ground rules. However, two of the most important points that one should observe when designing a user-interface are :

involve the user(s) (or potential user(s)) as much as possible to obtain feedback as to the usability of the system

use your commonsense!

9.2 Natural language
9.2.1 A simple system

Programming the computer to understand natural language (i.e. English) is a classic A.I. problem and one which is being extensively researched by the Japanese as part of their Fifth Generation Project. It is, as you might imagine, an extremely complex task and, so far, the systems which have been produced with natural language interfaces are capable only of recognising a restricted vocabulary concerned with a particular problem domain. The idealistic dream of being able to produce a system which can recognise, check the grammar of, and understand any English sentence which is typed in at its keyboard is still a long way in the future.

In fact, recognising natural language is a task which is non- trivial, even for human beings. When we have a conversation with another human being we tend to speak "in context". That is, each sentence that we speak is likely to be related to the context of the entire conversation and, thus, the sentences which have already been spoken. These sentences cannot, therefore, be taken sensibly in isolation as they may well become meaningless when taken out of the context of the current conversation.

It is a complex and difficult task to program a computer to undertake a conversation with a user in such a manner. The computer would need to be able to build up a dynamic model of the scenario surrounding each particular conversation, so that it could relate anything which was typed in by the user to that which had already been typed in earlier in that session.

It is not the intention of this section to try to outline methods of dealing with full natural language recognition. Rather, this and the following section of this chapter are intended to give the reader a flavour of the way in which Prolog can be employed in the design of some simple, prototype user interfaces which include some element of natural language recognition.

The elements of Prolog which have been covered in this book so far do allow us to build some form of simple intelligence into the interface of our programs. For example, consider the program below which instructs the computer to respond accordingly to user input phrased (rather clumsily) in the form of lists:

```
/* simple conversation system */

converse :- read(Inlist),
        response(Inlist,Outlist),
        write(Outlist),
        nl,
        converse.

response([],[]).
response([H|T],[L|M]) :- transform(H,L),
                         response(T,M).

transform(are,no).
transform(you,'I am').
transform(computer,person).
transform(man,woman).
transform(tired,awake).
transform(foolish,intelligent).
transform(intelligent,stupid).
transform(X,X).
```

129

The above program operates by using the top-level converse goal to read a list from the keyboard. It then proceeds to use the predicate response to convert the list which has been read into a suitable reply. The predicate response operates by first using the predicate transform to change the head of the input list into another word (according to the transform facts at the end of the program). Notice that if the word in the input list does not appear in any of the transform facts it is simply transformed into itself by the final "catch-all" fact transform(X,X). The response rule then calls itself recursively to transform the remainder (i.e. the tail) of the list. This process will continue until the input list has been reduced to the empty list, at which point the response goal will terminate and control will return to the converse rule. The converse rule will then write the list which has been created to the keyboard and wait for further input.

Notice that this program breaks one of the principles that was discussed earlier within this book - namely that of avoiding infinite recursion! The converse rule will recurse infinitely and the user will have to abort the program to halt it.

Running the above program will produce results of the form:

```
?- converse.
|: [are,you,a,computer].
[no,I am,a,person]
|: [are,you,a,man].
[no,I am,a,woman]
|: [are,you,foolish].
[no,I am,intelligent]
|: [are,you,intelligent].
[no,I am,stupid]
|: [are,you,tired].
[no,I am,awake].
|: [are,you,a,fool].
[no,I am,a,fool]
    .
    .
    .
etc.......
```

The above program provides a simple demonstration of the ability of Prolog to deal with natural language . This ability is demonstrated further in the following section of this chapter which describes a very simple natural language recognition system.

9.2.2 Natural language recognition

This section builds upon the transform program described in the previous section of this chapter to produce a Prolog program which can converse with its user in natural language (i.e. english). The program is essentially the same, but it has had an extra 'front end' added to it to cope with the natural language recognition.

The program operates in the following manner :

-   the user is required to enter a sentence in English

-   this is transformed into a list of Prolog objects

-   the list of Prolog objects is then fed to the transform program which produces a response as described in the previous section of this chapter

-   the output from transform is written in text form

The full Prolog program is shown below :

```
/* program to simulate a natural language
   question and answer session */

english :- nl,write('User > '),
        text(Inlist),nl,
        continue(Inlist).

/* english is the highest level predicate
   and controls the operation of the program

    - first it prompts the user and then  uses the
      predicate text to read in a natural language
      sentence and convert it into a list

    - the predicate continue then processes this list
*/

continue([finish,.]) :- !.

/* this is the stopping condition which terminates
   the program when the word finish is entered by
   the user */

continue(Inlist) :- response(Inlist,Outlist),
        write('Computer > '),
        print_list(Outlist),
        english.
```

```
/* continue will :

    - use the predicate response to create an answer
      (in the list Outlist) from the question posed by
      the user (which is in the list Inlist)

    - use the predicate print_list to print the answer
      in text form

    - recreate the english goal to continue the
      question and answer session */

text([Word|Words]) :- get0(Char),
      word(Char,Word,Char1),
      rest(Word,Char1,Words).

/* text will :

    - get the first character of the sentence

    - use word to read the first word of the sentence

    - and use rest to read the rest of the sentence

the entire sentence will be transformed into a list
*/

rest('.',_,[]) :- !.

  /* rest will terminate when a full stop is read */

rest(Word,Char,[Word1|Words]):-
word(Char,Word1,Char1),
rest(Word1,Char1,Words).

/* the recursive rest clause will :

  - read a word

  - recursively read the remainder of the sentence
*/

word(46,'.',_) :- !.

/* this version of word treats a full stop as a word
*/
```

```
word(Char,Word,Char2)  :- check(Char),!,
                          get0(Char1),
                          restw(Char1,Chars,Char2),
                          name(Word,[Char|Chars]).
```

/* this is the 'standard' version of word which
   will deal with the majority of words. It will :

  - check that the character is in the valid range

  - get0 the next character

  - use restw to read the rest of the word

  - use name to transform the word to list form */

```
word(Char,Word,Char2)  :- get0(Char1),
   word(Char1,Word,Char2).
```

/* this version of word is used to deal with the
   blanks (i.e. spaces) between words   */

```
restw(Char,[Char|Chars],Char2)  :- check(Char),!,
      get0(Char1),
      restw(Char1,Chars,Char2).
```

/* restw is used to read the remainder of a word */
```
restw(Char,[],Char).
```

/* this is the stopping condition which terminates
   restw when the blank character after the word is
   encountered */

```
check(Char)  :- Char > 96,
                Char < 123.
```

 /* check is used to check that the characters
   which make up a word are valid - only lower
   case letters are allowed */

```
response([],[]).
response([H|T],[L|M])  :- transform(H,L),
                          response(T,M).
```

/* the response predicate is used to generate
   an answer from the user's question */

```prolog
transform(are,no).
transform(you,'I am').
transform(computer,person).
transform(man,woman).
transform(tired,awake).
transform(foolish,intelligent).
transform(intelligent,stupid).
transform(how,' ').
transform(is,' ').
transform(weather,'weather is fine').
transform(what,' ').
transform(your,my).
transform(name,'name is Percy').
transform(i,' ').
transform(am,hello).
transform(X,X).
```

```prolog
/* the transform facts are used to change a
   word in the user's question to another
   word in the (computer's) answer

   - the final transform fact is a catch-all
   which simply changes any word which is
   not explicitly included in the list of
   facts into itself */
```

```prolog
print_list([])  :- nl.
print_list([H|T]) :- write(H),
                     tab(1),
                     print_list(T).
```

```prolog
/* print_list is used to print a list in text form

   - it works by writing the head of the list and
   then recursively print_listing the tail */
```

The type of dialogue which running this program will produce is shown below. As you will see, this program is still very much a prototype system, and a large amount of further work would be required to turn it into anything really useable. It does, however, serve to illustrate the ability of Prolog to deal with natural language recognition problems. It is this ability which makes Prolog an ideal language for the development of intelligent interfaces for both expert systems and intelligent database systems (which will allow the user to interrogate a conventional database by typing in english queries).

The user would first need to consult the file containing the english program and would then type the query :

134

```
?- english.
```

This would cause the following dialogue session to take place :

```
User > hello there.
Computer > hello there .
User > i am peter.
Computer >  hello peter .
User > what is your name.
Computer > my name is Percy .
User > are you a computer.
Computer > no I am a person .
User > are you intelligent.
Computer > no I am stupid .
User > how is the weather today.
Computer > the weather is fine today .
User > are you a man.
Computer > no I am a woman .
User > will you talk to me.
Computer > will I am talk to me .
```

By now the user might well be tiring of the rather inane nature of the computer's responses! However, losing your temper with such a system will not result in it providing you answers which are any more sensible. The session might continue as below:

```
User > are you foolish!.
Computer > no I am intelligent .
User > i do not think so.
Computer >  do not think so .
User > bye now.
Computer > bye now .
```

The session would finally be completed when the user types:

```
User > finish.
yes
```

Remaining with the subject of natural language recognition the following section of this chapter describes a high-level extension to the Prolog language (available only in certain versions of Prolog).

9.3 Grammar rules

Prolog provides a high-level grammar syntax which is designed for the processing of natural language. This is referred to as a 'high-level' syntax because it is, in fact, a kind of shorthand form of Prolog which is translated into full Prolog when the program is executed. The grammar facility allows you to define rules which can be applied to check the syntax of a sentence (or any other grammatical construct) as it is typed in by the user. It should be noted that not every version of the Prolog language provides the grammar facility as it is, in effect, an extension to standard Prolog.

Before considering an example which uses the grammar rule facility it will be useful to consider the rules of English grammar as they relate to a sentence. The structure of an English sentence is as defined in Figure 9.1 below:

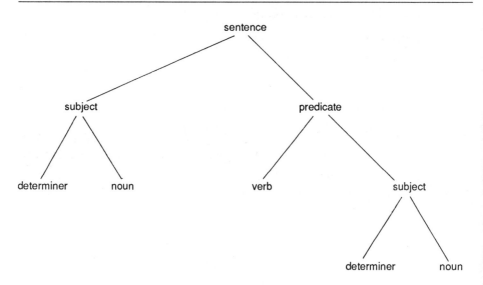

Fig. 9.1 The structure of an English sentence

In other words, a sentence (such as "the cat drinks the milk") consists of a subject ("the cat") and a predicate ("drinks the milk"). The subject of the sentence consists of a determiner ("the") and a noun ("cat"). The predicate consists of a verb ("drinks") and a subject, which in turn consists of a determiner ("the") and a noun ("milk").

To define such a grammar in Prolog terms one would write :

```
sentence  --> subject,predicate.
subject   --> determiner,noun.
predicate --> verb,subject.
```

where the symbol --> can be read to mean "consists of" and the comma in this case means "followed by" (rather than "and").

It is also necessary to provide a vocabulary to accompany our grammar. That is, we have to make a list of valid determiners, nouns and verbs such as that which follows :

```
determiner --> [the].
determiner --> [a].

noun --> [cat].
noun --> [dog].
noun --> [man].
noun --> [woman].
noun --> [milk].
noun --> [meat].
noun --> [bone].

verb --> [eats].
verb --> [drinks].
verb --> [hits].
verb --> [bites].
```

Prolog also provides a predicate, phrase, which can be used to check that a "phrase" is correct according to the rules that we have defined for our own particular grammar. A phrase is any grammatical construct which is acceptable according to those rules. The goal phrase(X,Y) succeeds if Y is a valid phrase of type X. For example, the goals

```
phrase(sentence, [the,cat,drinks,the,milk]).
phrase(sentence, [the,dog,eats,a,bone]).
phrase(subject, [the,man]).
phrase(predicate, [hits,the,dog]).
phrase(noun, [woman]).
phrase(verb, [eats]).
```

will all succeed. Notice, however, that the goal

```
phrase(sentence, [the,man,eats,the,bone]).
```

which is grammatically correct (but not very sensible) will also succeed! Notice also that the following goal, which contains a perfectly correct English sentence, will fail because the word "soup" has not been defined as part of the vocabulary.

```
phrase(sentence,[the,man,drinks,the,soup]).
```

The grammar rule system can thus be used to check the validity of sentences as they are typed in by the user. It can thus be an extremely useful component in the design of an intelligent user-interface.

9.4 Notes for Turbo Prolog programmers

Turbo Prolog provides several powerful facilities which can be used in the design of user-friendly software. These facilities include :

> string handling

> the use of windows

> graphics

> sound

This section presents a brief overview of some of the predicates which Turbo Prolog provides for introducing the above facilities into your software.

9.4.1 String handling

It should be noted that Turbo Prolog does not provide the grammar rule facility described in Section 9.3 . It does, however, provide extensive string handling facilities which can be used to manipulate text typed in by the user. The main predicates for string handling are explained below :

frontchar(S1,C,S2) - concatenates the character C and the string S2 to produce string S1. For example :

```
Goal: frontchar(X,'a',"bcd").
X=abcd
1 Solution
```

frontstr(N,S1,S2,S3) - splits S1 into two parts. N characters of S1 are stored in S2, and the rest in S3. For example :

```
Goal: frontstr(3,"hello",X,Y).
X=hel, Y=lo
1 Solution
```

fronttoken(S1,T,S2) - causes the concatenation of token T and string S2 to form string S1. A token is an object, character or string. For example :

```
Goal: fronttoken(X,fred,"xyz").
X=fredxyz
1 Solution
```

isname(S) - tests to see whether or not S is a valid object name. For example :

```
Goal:isname(john).
True
Goal: isname(x1).
True
```

str_len(S,L) - L is the length of string S. For example :

```
Goal: str_len(hello,L).
L=5
1 Solution
```

concat(S1,S2,S3) - concatenates strings S1 and S2 to produce S3. For example :

```
Goal: concat(ab,cd,X).
X=abcd
1 Solution
```

9.4.2 The use of windows

Turbo Prolog allows the user to create his own windows on the screen by using the predicates

makewindow – to create a window

shiftwindow – to move a window from one place on the screen to another

removewindow - to remove a window

clearwindow - to clear the contents of a window

The makewindow predicate is described briefly below :

makewindow(WindowNo,ScreenAttribute,FrameAttribute,Header,
Row,Column,Height,Width)

will create a window on the screen. The eight arguments of the makewindow predicate are defined below :

WindowNo - an integer number which is used to identify the window to Turbo Prolog

ScreenAttribute - an integer number which is used to specify background and foreground colours. For a monochrome display the number 7 is used to indicate white on black.

FrameAttribute - an integer number which is used to specify the colour of the border of the window. The integer 0 is used to specify that no border will be printed - any nonzero integer can be used to specify that a border should be printed on a monochrome display.

Header - a title which will be displayed at the top of the window.

Row, Column - these are integer values which are used to specify the row and column position of the top left hand corner of the window. (The top left hand corner of the entire screen is defined to be Row 0, Column 0 and the display size is usually 25 rows by 80 columns.)

Height, Width - these are integer values which are used to specify the dimensions of the window.

For example, the command

```
makewindow(1,7,7,"Example Window",10,10,15,15)
```

defines window number 1, for a monochrome display unit. The window will have a border and will be titled "Example Window". It will be square, 15 rows high and wide and will be positioned with its top left hand corner at row 10, column 10 of the display.

These powerful window handling facilities are described in full in the Turbo Prolog user manual.

9.4.3 Graphics and sound

Turbo Prolog also allows the user to make full use of the graphics and sound facilities available on the IBM PC. For further details of the use of these facilities the user should consult the Turbo Prolog manual.

Chapter 10

DEVELOPING AN EXPERT SYSTEM

10.1 Introduction

This chapter is devoted to coverage of the development, in Prolog, of a small expert system. Although the system under consideration here is too limited to be considered a realistic expert system, the principles covered, and the way in which the system is structured and operates, are entirely similar to those which apply to much larger and practical expert systems. The content of this chapter is, therefore, designed to give the reader a clear understanding of the way in which a full blown expert system would be developed.

Indeed, it is quite true to say that the concepts of expert systems can often be demonstrated by the use of relatively simple examples, as the translation from smaller scale systems to much larger, and more realistic systems, often involves very few changes to the general structure of the knowledge base and, hence the operation of the program. That is, the major difference between small example systems and real-world systems is the number of facts and rules contained in the knowledge base and not the philosophy behind, or the construction of, the expert system.

The system which is described in this chapter is an example of one of the most common forms of expert systems; namely, that type of system which is designed to enable the user to identify a particular item, object or entity. Such systems are termed, for obvious reasons, identification systems.

10.2 The identification problem

Many expert systems are based upon the concept of identification. That is, the expertise or knowledge which they contain is concerned with the identification of a particular item, object, or entity. Such systems may be employed for the identification of objects (or, indeed, anything!) from many different fields, such as the examples outlined below:

A geological expert system for rock identification. The knowledge base of such a system would contain rules relating to such properties as the thickness, colour, weight and strength of rocks.

A chemical expert system for use in the identification of chemical compounds.The knowledge base of this system would contain rules relating to such chemical properties as atomic mass and structure, in addition to more straightforward properties such as the colour of the compound and whether it is a liquid or a solid form.

A medical expert system for the diagnosis (i.e. identification) of particular illnesses. The knowledge base of this system would contain facts and rules relating to the symptoms which a patient would exhibit if he were suffering from certain diseases.

The vast majority of identification systems are structured in a similar manner and operate according to a similar set of principles. It is the intention of this chapter to provide the reader with an understanding of these principles.

Typically, an identification system will ask the user of the system a series of questions which have been carefully designed to elicit information for identification purposes. The system will continually match the user's responses with the facts and rules in the knowledge base until enough information has been obtained to enable a positive identification to be made. (Alternatively, the system also needs to ask enough questions in order to be sure that it cannot successfully identify the item in question!).

Such an expert system will employ an interactive question and answer session for the purpose of learning about the particular object or item which the user wishes to identify. When the system has learnt enough for identification purposes it will inform the user as to the identity of the object.

The particular identification problem described in this chapter is based upon the classification of pedigree dogs. That is, the expert system has embodied within it knowledge relating to pedigree dogs so that, given any dog contained within the knowledge base, the system will ask the user a series of questions until that dog is positively identified.

The knowledge engineering process in this particular example would probably be quite straightforward, in that the required information and expertise relating to pedigree dogs is quite readily obtainable from books on the subject. However, it is not inconceivable that the knowledge engineer might approach an expert on pedigree dogs in order to obtain more detailed information, particularly in relation to the less common, and more unusual breeds of dog.

The knowledge implanted within the expert system is based upon the grouping system employed by the Kennel Club of Great Britain. This grouping system places any pedigree dog into one of six possible groups. The six groups are :

Hounds. These are hunting dogs which trail by sight or scent.
Gun dogs. These are dogs which, in general, accompany hunters who are hunting game birds. Such dogs will often be used for retrieving the dead bird which has been shot by the hunter.

Terriers. These are dogs which are particularly adept at digging. They are, as a result, used for ferretting out animals such as rabbits, badgers and foxes.

Working dogs. As the name suggests these are dogs which are bred largely for work purposes. That is, working dogs are used to help man by performing such tasks as herding cattle, guarding property, saving lost travellers and pulling sleighs.

Toy dogs. These are very small dogs which are bred as pets.

Utilities. Dogs which do not fit into any of the above categories are classed as utilities by the Kennel Club. Generally speaking, utilities are medium sized pet dogs.

The example system described in the following sections of this chapter is based upon the above six groupings and includes three dogs from each Kennel Club grouping. Obviously, this is a very restricted system, as the number of dogs in each grouping is considerably larger than three. However, the structure of the system and the philosophy behind its development would not alter if it were to be extended to include a much larger, and hence more realistic, set of pedigree dogs. The full classification system included in the expert system is depicted in Figure 10.1.

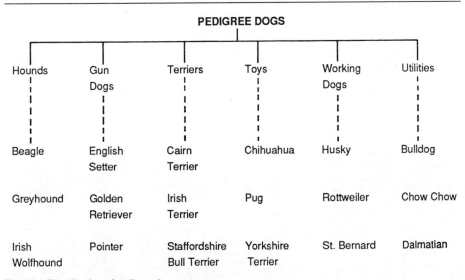

Fig. 10.1 Classification of pedigree dogs

10.3 Setting up the expert system

Before considering in detail the development of the dog identification expert system (which we will henceforth refer to as "dogs" for convenience), we will first discuss the way in which one might approach the design of "large" Prolog programs ("large" meaning more involved than the programs which have been covered so far in this text). The following section is designed to cover this aspect of Prolog program design.

10.3.1 Top down design

When developing an expert system, and indeed any Prolog program, it is often easier if one proceeds in what is known in Computer Science as a "top-down manner", according to the principle of "top-down design". The principle of top-down design is :

Start with the initial problem and break that problem down into a series of stages. Then proceed to successively refine each of these stages until you have reached the stage where the problems which you have can be easily expressed in a programming language (i.e. Prolog in our case).

This principle is based upon the simple concept of "divide and conquer" which states that it is easier to solve a problem by breaking it down into smaller stages than to try to consider the problem in its entirety. For instance, consider the simple example shown in Figure 10.2 which demonstrates diagrammatically how an initial goal which consists of the problem :

calculate the average of a list of numbers

may be broken down in a top-down fashion.

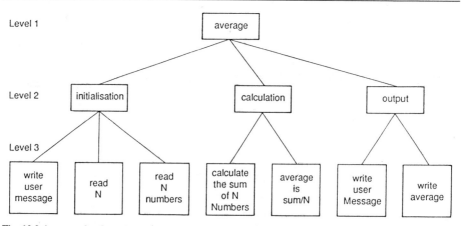

Fig. 10.2 An example of top-down design

The chart in Figure 10.2 shows how the initial goal (denoted "average") is subdivided into three subgoals:

> **initialisation** - this goal is designed to provide the user of the program with instructions as to its use, and read in the lists of numbers which are to be averaged
> **calculation** - this goal performs the calculations needed to compute the average of the list of numbers
> **output** - this goal displays the result of the program

Each of these goals is then, in turn, subdivided into its constituent subgoals until the entries in the chart are in a form which can easily be written in Prolog. The Prolog program which was designed in this manner is shown below :

```
average:- init(N,List),
          calc(N,List,Ave),
          output(Ave).

/* the head of this rule corresponds to
   level 1 of the chart in Fig 10.2 */

init(N,List)  :- nl,nl,
write('Program to calculate the average'),nl,
write('of a list of numbers'),nl,nl,
write('How many numbers ? '),
read(N),nl,
write('Now type in '),write(N),
write(' numbers '),nl,nl,
input(N,List).

calc(N,List,Ave)  :- sum(List,Sum),
Ave is Sum / N.

output(Ave)  :- nl,nl,
          write('the average of your numbers is '),
          write(Ave),
          nl,nl.

/* the heads of these rules correspond to
   level 2 of the chart in Fig. 10.2 */

input(0,[])  :- !.
input(N,[H|T])  :- read(H),
                   M is N - 1,
                   input(M,T).

sum([],0)  :- !.
sum([H|T],S)  :- sum(T,S1),
                 S is H + S1.
```

The principle of top-down design can prove to be very useful in the design of Prolog programs. The following section describes how the dogs system is developed in a top-down fashion.

10.3.2 Development of the 'dogs' expert system

This section describes in detail the way in which the dogs expert system is developed. The basic structure of the system is shown in diagrammatic form in Figure 10.3.

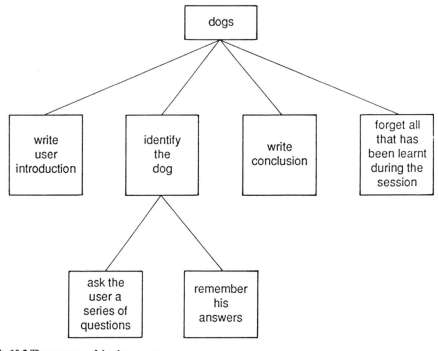

Fig 10.3 The structure of the dogs system

The top-level goal of the dogs system can be expressed in the form :

```
dogs :- init,
        identify(Dog),
        out_message(Dog),
        forget.
```

This top-level goal is simply stating that the entire program dogs consists of four subgoals; namely :

init - which displays instructional messages to inform the user as to the purpose and operation of the program.

identify - which attempts to identify the user's Dog.

out_message - which displays the closing messages to the user. These will include the name of the Dog (if it has been successfully identified) or a message which states that the system cannot identify the user's Dog.

forget - this goal makes sure that the system forgets all that it has learnt about the

146

user's Dog. This is necessary so that it will not confuse it with the next Dog to be identified.

Each of the above four subgoals will be discussed in more detail below. The full program listing of the dogs system is shown in Section 10.4 of this chapter.

10.3.2.1 init

This goal requires little further explanation. Basically it will consist of a series of write goals which will display some instructional text for the user.

10.3.2.2 identify

The identify goal is the main driving force of the program. In fact, there will be 19 versions of the identify rule, one for each of the 18 dogs in the system, and one which will be used if all of the previous 18 have failed and the dog cannot, therefore, be identified. Examples of two identify rules are given below :

```
identify(beagle)  :- group(hound),
                     appearance(muscular),
                     appearance(compact),
                     resemble(snoopy).

identify(rottweiler)  :- group('working dog'),
                         appearance(muscular),
                         appearance(solid),
                         appearance(strong),
                         appearance(powerful),
                         coat(coarse),
                         coat(thick),
                         coat(dark),
                         does(guarding).
```

As you can see, both of these identify rules have a similar structure (as will all of the first 18 identify rules in the program). That is, they first state to which group the dog belongs, and then proceed to list a series of attributes relating to that dog. For instance, the above two rules could be expressed in English as:

"The beagle belongs to the hound group, has a muscular and compact appearance and resembles Snoopy."

"The rottweiler belongs to the working dog group, and has a muscular, solid, strong and powerful appearance. It has a coarse, thick, dark coat and is used for guarding."

When it encounters an 'identify' goal Prolog will search through the knowledge base trying each identify rule in turn in an attempt to prove that the dog in question belongs to the correct group and fits the attributes listed in the body of the rule. In order to do so we must design the program so that it asks the user a series of questions. For instance, consider the following group rules :

```
group(Group)   :- is_fact(group,Group),!.

group(Group)   :- is_not(group,Group),!,fail.

group(Group)   :- not(is_fact(group,_)),nl,
                  group_message(Group,Mess),
                  write('Is it a '),
                  write(Mess),
                  write(' ? '),
                  read(Response),
                  act_on(Response,group,Group).
```

The first of these group rules is stating that the program has already learnt (as a result of the user's answer to a previous question), that the dog belongs to that particular group. That is, the goal

```
is_fact(group,Group).
```

is stating that it is a fact that the group of the dog is that which is held in the variable Group.

The second of the group rules is stating the converse of the first. That is, it is saying that the system has already learnt that the dog is definitely not a member of that particular group.

The final group rule will only come into play if the system still does not know whether or not the dog is a member of that group. In this situation the system will first use the goal

```
not(is_fact(group,_))
```

to ensure that the dog has not already been identified as belonging to another group. Obviously, if it has been, there is no point in trying to prove that it belongs to any other group, as a dog cannot belong to more than one group! The system will then use the group_message clause to find a message relating to that dog grouping and will then ask the user a question based on that message. For example, the group hound might have a group_message clause of the form :

```
group_message(hound,'hunting dog that tracks by
sight or scent').
```

which would result in the question :

```
Is it a hunting dog that tracks by sight or scent ?
```

being displayed. The user will answer either yes or no to such a question, and his response will be processed by the goal act_on. If he responds yes the program will then assert an is_fact clause to state that the dog is a member of that group. If he responds no the program will assert an is_not clause to state that the dog is definitely not a member of that group. In this mannner the program ensures that it learns from user's responses to the questions which it asks and, hence, never has to ask the same question twice.

The act_on predicate takes the form :

```
act_on(yes,Attribute,Type)  :-
asserta(is_fact(Attribute,Type)).

act_on(no,Attribute,Type)  :-
asserta(is_not(Attribute,Type)),fail.
```

where the first of the two act_on rules is used to assert that it is a fact that the dog possesses a particular Type of Attribute. The second of the two rules is stating the converse of this; that is, that the dog definitely does not possess that particular type of Attribute.

The above discussion has described how the group to which a dog belongs may be determined by the system. The principle for developing the rules to determine the other attributes of a dog are essentially the same. The interested reader may wish to turn to Section 10.4 of this chapter at this point, where these rules are listed in full.

Finally, it is necessary to design a version of the identify rule which will be used if the system has failed to match the dog with any of the previous 18 identify rules. This can simply take the form :

```
identify(no)  :- !.
```

The above clause will simply instantiate the variable Dog to the value "no" if no appropriate match has been found earlier in its search through the knowledge base.

10.3.2.3 out_message

This goal is intended to display the name of the dog which the system has identified. It will be necessary to have two versions of this rule; one which will be used if the dog has been positively identified, and one which will be used if the system has failed to identify the dog. These two versions of out_message will take the form :

```
out_message(no)  :- !,nl,nl,
  write('*********************************'),
  nl,nl,
  write('Failure !'),nl,nl,
  write('I cannot identify your dog.'),
  nl,nl.

out_message(Dog)  :- nl,nl,
  write('*********************************'),
  nl,nl,
  write('Your dog is a(n) '),
  write(Dog),
  nl,nl.
```

10.3.2.4 forget

The purpose of this goal is perhaps less obvious at first sight than might be the case
with the previous three goals which have been discussed. Remember, however, that the
operation of identify involves the system learning (i.e. asserting) facts about the
attribute of a particular dog; these facts having been deduced from the user's responses
to a series of questions. If the program is then to be run again for another dog, the facts
which have been asserted will no longer apply. For this reason, it is necessary to
instruct Prolog to forget all which it has learned during its question and answer session
with the dogs user. This is achieved by retracting the is_fact and is_not clauses. The
form of forget will, therefore, be :

```
forget :- retract(is_fact(Attribute,Type)),fail.

forget :- retract(is_not(Attribute,Type)),fail.

forget :- nl,
          write(' Program finished. '),
          nl,nl.
```

10.4 Full program listing

This section contains a full listing of the 'dogs' expert system. The program listed here
is identical to that described in the previous section of this chapter in all but one
respect. The program listed here has been modified so that after having run once, it will
request the user whether or not he wishes to run the program for another dog. It is left
to the interested reader to pick out the changes to the structure of the program which
have resulted from this modification.

```
/* program to identify pedigree dogs according
   to groupings of the Kennel Club, Great Britain */

dogs :- init,dogs1.

dogs1 :- identify(Dog),
         out_message(Dog),
         forget.

/* dogs is the top-level predicate which controls
   the operation of the program */

init :- nl,nl,
        write('This is a program to identify'),nl,
        write('pedigree dogs, according to the'),nl,
        write('groupings of the Kennel Club'),nl,
        write('of Great Britain.'),nl,nl,
        write('The program will ask a series'),nl,
        write('of questions to which you must'),nl,
        write('answer yes or no .'),nl,nl,
        write('The program will attempt to'),nl,
        write('identify your dog. '),nl,nl,
        write('Press return key to continue : '),
        get0(_),nl,nl.

/* init displays introductory text */

identify(beagle) :- group(hound),
                    appearance(muscular),
                    appearance(compact),
                    resemble(snoopy).

identify(greyhound) :- group(hound),
                       appearance(muscular),
                       coat(short),
                       does(racing).

identify('Irish wolfhound') :- group(hound),
                               appearance(muscular),
                               coat(short),
                               does(racing).

identify('English setter') :- group('gun dog'),
                              appearance('medium
                              height'),
                              coat(long),
                              coat(silky).
```

```
identify('golden retriever') :- group('gun dog'),
                      appearance('medium height'),
                      coat(golden),
                      muzzle(wide).

identify(pointer) :- group('gun dog'),
                   appearance(muscular),
                   coat(short),
                   muzzle(long).

identify('Cairn terrier') :- group(terrier),
                         appearance(small),
                         appearance(compact),
                         appearance(hardy),
                         coat(rough).

identify('Irish terrier') :- group(terrier),
                         appearance(small),
                         appearance(hardy),
                         coat(hard),
                         coat(wiry).

identify('Staffordshire bull terrier') :-
                      group(terrier),
                      appearance(small),
                      coat(short),
                      coat(soft).

identify(chihuahua) :-group(toy),
                    appearance('extremely small'),
                    coat(short).

identify(pug) :- group(toy),
              appearance(compact),
              appearance('square shaped'),
              muzzle('short and blunt').

identify('Yorkshire terrier'):- group(toy),
                             appearance(compact),
                             muzzle(short),
                             coat(long),
                             coat(shiny).

identify(husky) :- group('working dog'),
                 appearance(strong),
                 coat(soft),
                 coat(downy),
                 does('sleigh pulling').
```

```prolog
identify(rottweiler) :- group('working dog'),
                        appearance(muscular),
                        appearance(solid),
                        appearance(strong),
                        appearance(powerful),
                        coat(coarse),
                        coat(thick),
                        coat(dark),
                        does(guarding).

identify('Saint Bernard') :- group('working dog'),
                        appearance(muscular),
                        appearance(tall),
                        coat(thick),
                        does('saving lost
                        travellers').

identify(bulldog) :- group(utility),
                     appearance(stocky),
                     appearance(low),
                     appearance(compact),
                     coat(fine),
                     coat(short),
                     coat(red).

identify('chow chow') :- group(utility),
                         appearance(massive),
                         coat(thick),
                         coat(woolly),
                         coat(red).

identify(dalmatian) :- group(utility),
                       appearance(muscular),
                       appearance(tall),
                       coat(short),
                       coat(fine),
                       coat('white, black spotted').

identify(no) :- !.

/* the identify rules are used to identify
particular dogs by their group and attributes */

group(Group) :- is_fact(group,Group),!.
group(Group) :- is_not(group,Group),!,fail.
group(Group) :- not(is_fact(group,_)),nl,
```

153

```
        group_message(Group,Mess),
        write('Is it a '),
        write(Mess),
        write(' ? '),
        read(Response),
        act_on(Response,group,Group).

/* the group rules are used to determine the group
   to which a dog belongs */

group_message(hound,'hunting dog that tracks by
sight or scent').
group_message('gun dog','dog which accompanies a
game-hunter').
group_message(terrier,'digging dog').
group_message(toy,'very small pet').
group_message('working dog','dog bred for working').
group_message(utility,'medium to large pet').

/* the group message facts contain output messages
   for each group */

appearance(Type) :- is_fact(appearance,Type),!.
appearance(Type) :- is_not(appearance,Type),!,fail.
appearance(Type) :- nl,
     write('Is it a '),
     write(Type),
     write(' dog ? '),
     read(Response),
     act_on(Response,appearance,Type).

resemble(Type) :- is_fact(resemble,Type),!.
resemble(Type) :- is_not(resemble,Type),!,fail.
resemble(Type) :- nl,
        write('Does it resemble '),
        write(Type),
        write(' ? '),
        read(Response),
        act_on(Response,resemble,Type).

coat(Type) :- is_fact(coat,Type),!.
coat(Type) :- is_not(coat,Type),!,fail.
coat(Type) :- nl,
        write('Does it have a '),
        write(Type),
        write(' coat ? '),
```

```prolog
        read(Response),
        act_on(Response,coat,Type).

does(Work) :- is_fact(does,Work),!.
does(Work) :- is_not(does,Work),!,fail.
does(Work) :- nl, write('Is it used for '),
        write(Work),
        write(' ? '),
        read(Response),
        act_on(Response,does,Work).

muzzle(Type) :- is_fact(muzzle,Type),!.
muzzle(Type) :- is_not(muzzle,Type),!,fail.
muzzle(Type) :- nl,
        write('Does it have a '),
        write(Type),
        write(' muzzle ? '),
        read(Response),
        act_on(Response,muzzle,Type).
```

/* the appearance, resemble, coat, does and muzzle
rules identify attributes of a given dog */

```prolog
act_on(yes,Attribute,Type) :-
        asserta(is_fact(Attribute,Type)).

act_on(no,Attribute,Type) :-
        asserta(is_not(Attribute,Type)),fail.
```

/* the act_on clauses enable the system to learn
  from the user's responses */

```prolog
out_message(no) :- !,nl,nl,
    write('***********************************'),
    nl,nl,
    write('Failure !'),nl,nl,
    write('I cannot identify your dog.'), nl,nl.

out_message(Dog) :- nl,nl,
    write('***********************************'),
    nl,nl,
    write('Your dog is a(n) '),
    write(Dog),nl,nl.
```

/* out_message is used to display the system's
conclusions */

```
forget :- retract(is_fact(Attribute,Type)),fail.
forget :- retract(is_not(Attribute,Type)),fail.
forget :- nl,
        write(' Program finished. '),nl,nl,redo.

/* forget is used to clear the knowledge base for
   the next run of the program */

redo :- write('Run the program again ? '),
        read(Response),
        run_again(Response).

run_again(yes) :- nl,nl,
        dogs1.

run_again(no)  :- nl,nl.

/* redo and run_again are used to enable the
user to run the program again if he so desires */
```

10.5 Using the system

This section demonstrates how the dogs system can be used to identify three pedigree dogs : a greyhound, a rottweiler and a chihuahua. In order to use the dogs system it would be necessary to first enter Prolog and then consult the file containing the system. Having done so, the user would enter the command :

```
?- dogs.
```

This would result in the following text being displayed at his terminal :

```
This is a program to identify
pedigree dogs, according to the
groupings of the Kennel Club
of Great Britain.

The program will ask you a series
of questions to which you must
answer yes or no .

The program will then attempt to
identify your dog.

Press the return key to continue :
```
After pressing the return key the system would present the user with a series of

questions, to which he must reply yes or no. The following question and answer session would result:

```
Is it a hunting dog that tracks by sight or scent?
yes.

Is it a muscular dog ? yes.
Is it a compact dog ? no.
Does it have a short coat ? yes.
Is it used for racing ? yes.


* * * * * * * * * * * * * * * * * * * * * * * * * * * * * * * * * * * * *


Your dog is a(n) greyhound
Program finished.

Do you wish to run the program again ? yes.
```

The user has now indicated that he wishes to run the program again in order to identify another dog. As he has already seen the initial instructions the first time that he ran the program, these will not be displayed again. The system will, therefore, simply begin by questioning the user in a similar manner to before :

```
Is it a hunting dog that tracks by sight or scent ?
no.
Is it a dog which accompanies a game-hunter ? no.
Is it a digging dog ? no.
Is it a very small pet ? no.
Is it a dog bred for working ? yes.
Is it a strong dog ? yes.
Does it have a soft coat ? no.
Is it a muscular dog ? yes.
Is it a solid dog ? yes.
Is it a powerful dog ? yes.
Does it have a coarse coat ? yes.
Does it have a thick coat ? yes.
Does it have a dark coat ? yes.
Is it used for guarding ? yes.


* * * * * * * * * * * * * * * * * * * * * * * * * * * * * * * * * * * * *


Your dog is a(n) rottweiler

Program finished.
Do you wish to run the program again ? yes.
```

```
Is it a hunting dog that tracks by sight or scent ?
no.
Is it a dog which accompanies a game-hunter ? no.
Is it a digging dog ? no.
Is it a very small pet ? yes.
Is it a extremely small dog ? yes.
Does it have a short coat ? yes.


************************************

Your dog is a(n) chihuahua

Program finished.

Do you wish to run the program again ? yes.
```

The following dialogue demonstrates the way in which the system copes when it cannot positively identify the user's dog :

```
Is it a hunting dog that tracks by sight or scent ?
yes.
Is it a muscular dog ? no.

************************************

Failure !
I cannot identify your dog.
Program finished.
```

In this case the system cannot identify the dog because all of the hounds which it has stored in its knowledge base are muscular. Once again the system asks the user if he wishes to run the program again.

```
Do you wish to run the program again ? yes.

Is it a hunting dog that tracks by sight or scent ?
no.
Is it a dog which accompanies a game-hunter ? no.
Is it a digging dog ? yes.
Is it a small dog ? no.

************************************

Failure !
I cannot identify your dog.
Program finished.
```

10.6 Extending the system to one which learns

Every really useful expert system must have the capacity to learn. That is, the system must be able to extend its knowledge base to include new facts and rules about its own particular problem domain. The example dogs system should be no exception. Indeed, as at the moment the system contains a very limited amount of expertise (limited to 18 dogs, to be precise) it would seem rather silly if it could not be extended to include additional knowledge!

Ideally the system should be able to be extended by a human expert, or a user. That is, it should not require a knowledge engineer to add every little extra piece of knowledge. Also, it should not be necessary to change the Prolog code manually to include extra facts and/or rules. Rather, the Prolog code should be able to modify itself.

This extra capability can easily be achieved by adding an extra learning component to the dogs system. This component will then be run by the user when he wishes to add the details of another dog to the knowledge base. The Prolog program for such a learning system would take the form shown below:

```
learn :- set_up,
         dialog.

/* learn is the top-level goal which controls
   the operation of the program */

set_up :- nl,nl,
  write('This program will enable you to add'),nl,
  write('another dog to the knowledge base'),
  nl,nl.

/* set_up displays an introductory user message */

dialog :- write('What is the name of the dog ? '),
  read(Name),nl,
  write('To which group does it belong ? '),
  read(Group),nl,
  write('Name a feature of its appearance : '),
  read(App1),nl,
  write('Name another feature of its appearance : '),
  read(App2),nl,
  write('Name a feature of its coat : '),
  read(Coat),nl,
  write('I will remember that ! '),nl,nl,
  remember(Name,Group,App1,App2,Coat).
```

```
/* dialog asks the user to enter information about
the dog which he wishes to add to the system */

remember(Name,Group,App1,App2,Coat) :-
 asserta((identify(Name) :- group(Group),
 appearance(App1),
 appearance(App2),
 coat(Coat))).

/* remember adds this information to the system by
   asserting a new identify rule */
```

This learning system restricts the user in the way in which he may add information relating to a particular dog. The information which he must supply for his new dog is :

the name of the dog's breed
the group to which the dog belongs
two pieces of information relating to the dog's appearance
one piece of information concerning the dog's coat.

So, for example, if the user wished to add a pekingese to the dogs system, he would run the learning system in the manner shown below:

```
?- learn.

This program will enable you to add
another dog to the knowledge base

What is the name of the dog ? pekingese.
To which group does it belong ? toy.
Name a feature of its appearance : solid.
Name another feature of its appearance : alert.
Name a feature of its coat : long.

I will remember that !
```

This would result in the following additional identify rule being included within the knowledge base :

```
identify(pekingese) :- group(toy) ,
           appearance(solid),
           appearance(alert),
           coat(long).
```

The dogs system could then be used to identify a pekingese as shown be the terminal session shown below:

```
Is it a very small pet ? yes.
Is it a solid dog ? yes.
Is it a alert dog ? yes.
Does it have a long coat ? yes.


**************************************

Your dog is a(n) pekingese
Program finished.
```

The learning system shown here would , however, only "remember" the new knowledge which it has gained for the duration of the current Prolog session. That is, as soon as the user leaves Prolog this knowledge would be lost. This situation could easily be changed by including a section in the learning program to save the new rules on disc. This could be achieved by writing the rules to a file. The knowledge engineer in charge of the system could then examine the new rules in the file and decide whether or not they should be included as a permanent feature of the system. In this way, it could be ensured that no "corruption of the knowledge base" (whether deliberate or otherwise) could take place. Such a measure is obviously extremely important in commercial expert systems where the reliability of the system may be vital.

10.7 Making the system explain its conclusions

It is generally accepted that, if an expert system is to have any hope of being accepted by both expert and non-expert users, it must be able to explain the logic behind its answers. That is, the system must be able to show the user which rule(s) it is using in order to come to its conclusions. The dogs system can quite easily be modified to provide such explanation facilities. This is achieved by modifying the out_message predicate to include an additional explain facility as shown below :

```
out_message(X)  :- nl,
        write('Your dog is a(n) '),
        write(X),
        nl,nl,
        explain(X),
        nl,nl.

explain(Dog)  :- write('The following attributes'),
        write('were used'),nl,
        write('to identify your dog : '),nl,nl,
        clause(identify(Dog),Body),
        write(Body).
```

The dogs system would now operate in the following manner :

```
Is it a hunting dog that tracks by sight or scent ?
no.
Is it a dog which accompanies a game-hunter ? no.
Is it a digging dog ? yes.
Is it a small dog ? yes.
Is it a compact dog ? yes.
Is it a hardy dog ? yes.
Does it have a rough coat ? yes.

Your dog is a(n) Cairn terrier

The following attributes were used
to identify your dog :

group(terrier),appearance(small),appearance(compact)
,appearance(hardy),coat(rough)

Program finished.
```

10.8 Summary

This chapter has presented, in some detail an example of one particular form of expert system; namely, an identification system. The main identification mechanisms have been covered, as have the ways in which the system can be extended to learn new knowledge and to explain the logic behind its conclusions. To summarise it is true to say that the majority of expert systems are likely to possess similar components to those described in this chapter (and first hinted at in chapter 1). That is, the system will comprise:

a user interface
an inference engine (in the case of this chapter the inference engine has been the identification system)
a knowledge base
knowledge acquisition tools (i.e. the learning system)
the ability to explain its findings

A more detailed diagram of a generalised expert system is shown in Figure 10.4, overleaf.

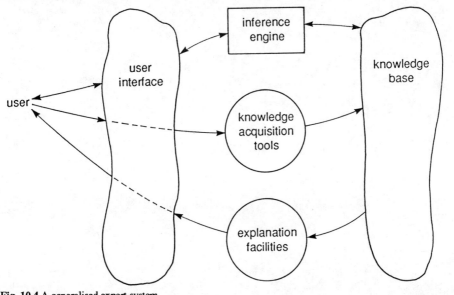

Fig. 10.4 A generalised expert system

Chapter 11

Case Studies

11.1 Introduction

In order to further illustrate the role of Prolog in the design of expert systems, and to provide the reader with some more advanced examples of Prolog programming, this chapter is devoted entirely to the study of a series of case studies. Each case study represents the design of a "mini" expert system and has been divided into four sections, namely :

definition of the problem area

a full Prolog program listing

notes relating to the program

a sample terminal session

The case studies have been chosen from several different subject areas but are designed to be comprehensible to the general reader who has no specialised knowledge of that particular problem area.

11.2 A pub guide for tourists

11.2.1 The problem

The tourist information centre in Anytown is currently investigating new ways of providing information to visitors to the town. They have just invested in a microcomputer system and are trying to make as much use of it as possible. They have decided, therefore, to ask a local software house to devise a system which can be used by tourists in order to obtain information regarding the public houses in the town.

The type of service which they wish the system to provide is:

To enable a visitor to identify which public houses are in particular areas of the town. This option will work by allowing the user to choose an area of the town - the system will then list all of the pubs in that area. Thus a tourist who is staying at an hotel in a particular part of town can quickly find out which pubs are close at hand.

To enable a tourist to identify which pubs have certain amenities. This option will allow the user to choose an amenity (e.g. restaurant, accommodation, music) - the system will then list the pubs which possess that particular amenity.

To allow the tourist to find the amenities available at a particular pub. This option will ask the user to type in the name of a particular pub - the system will then list the amenities available at that pub.

It is intended that the system should be readily useable by the average man in the street.

11.2.2 Full program listing

```
/* a pub guide for tourists */

pubguide :- nl,nl,
            write('The following options are available:'),
            nl,nl,nl,nl,
            write(' To find which pubs are in each area
            of Anytown'),tab(10),write('1'),nl,
            write('To find which pubs have certain
            amenities'),
            tab(15),write('2'),nl,
            write('To find the amenities available at a
            given pub'),tab(10),write('3'),
            nl,nl,nl,nl,
            write('Enter option 1 , 2 or 3 '),
            nl,nl,
            read(Opt),
            option(Opt).

/* pubguide is the top-level predicate and implements
   the initial menu */

option(1) :- nl,
            write(Areas of Anytown'),
            nl,nl,nl,
            areas(Arealist),
            write_menu(Arealist,1),nl,nl,
            write('Type in a number to choose a particular
                   area '),nl,nl,
            read(Areano),
            option1(Areano).
```

```
/* the first version of the option predicate implements
the first option on the initial menu */

option1(areano) :- nl,
                write('List of pubs in '),
                areanumb(Area,Areano),
                write(Area),write(' area'),
                nl,nl,nl,
                pub(Area,Pub,Amenity),
                write(Pub),nl,
                fail.

/* the option1 predicate lists the pubs in
a particular area */
option(2) :- nl,
                write('List of Amenities'),
                nl,nl,nl,
                amenities(Amenlist),
                write_menu(Amenlist,1),
                nl,nl,
                write('Type a number to choose an amenity'),
                nl,nl,
                read(Ameno),
                option2(Ameno).

/* the second version of the option predicate implements
the second option on the initial menu */
option2:meno) :- nl,
                write('List of pubs with '),
                amenumb(Amenity,Ameno)
                write(Amenity),
                nl,nl,nl,
                pub(Area,Pub,Amenlist),
                member(Amenity,Amenlist),
                write(Pub),nl,
                fail.

/* the option2 predicate finds and lists all of the
  pubs with a specified amenity */

option(3) :- nl,
                write('Amenities available at a given pub'),
                nl,nl,nl,
                write('Type in name of pub'),
                nl,nl,
                read(Pub),
```

```prolog
            nl,nl,
            pub(Area,Pub,Amenlist),
            write_list(Amenlist).
```

/* the third version of the option predicate implements
the third option on the initial menu */

```prolog
write_menu([],_).
write_menu([H|T],I) - write(H),tab(10),write(I),
                   nl,J is I + 1,
                   write_menu(T,J).
```

/* the write_menu predicate is used to write a list
   in the form of a menu */

```prolog
write_list([]).
write_list[H|T]) :- write(H),nl,
                  write_list(T).
```

/* write_list will write a list with each element
   on a new line */

```prolog
member(X, [X|_]).
member(:[_|Y]) :- member(X,Y).
```


```prolog
areas(['town_centre ',warwick_road,paddock_lane).
```

/* list of areas of Anytown */


```prolog
amenities(['restaurant ','music ',accommodation]).
```

/* list of amenities covered by the system */

```prolog
pub(town_centre,red_lion,[restaurant,music]).
pub(town_centre,black_horse,[music]).
pub(warwick_road,kings_head,[accommodation,restaurant]).
pub(warwick_road,sailors_rest,[music]).
pub(warwick_road,four_pennies,[]).
pub(paddock_lane,castles,[restaurant]).
pub(paddock_lane,legionnaire,[music]).
```

/* list of pub facts - pub(X,Y,Z) is in area X ,
   has name Y and amenities Z */

11.2.3 Notes

The pubguide program is a simple example of a menu driven expert system which the reader who has studied the contents of this book should have little trouble understanding. There are, however, a number of points which are worthy of mention.

The program is intended to be useable by the average "man in the street" and hence the menus have been designed to be as easy to use as possible. User responses have been restricted to integer values as far as possible. The one exception to this is when the user is asked to request details of a particular pub. It would obviously be extremely cumbersome to list all of the pubs in the database (especially if it were of a realistic size) with their accompanying option numbers. The designer is, therefore, left with little option but to ask the user to type in the name of the pub which he wishes to ask the system about.

The write_menu predicate is designed to write a list of elements in the form of a menu. That is, each of the elements in the list is written on a new line with an accompanying option number. For instance, the goal

```
write_menu(List,1)
```

will cause the elements of the list List to be written out with the first element of the list having option number 1. The following elements of the list will each be on new lines and will be numbered 2 , 3 , 4 etc.

The actual database of facts concerning areas, pubs and amenities is, to say the least, somewhat brief. A full working pub guide system would probably contain at least ten times as many such facts. The database in the above program is, however, sufficient for the purposes of a case study.

11.2.4 Sample terminal session

```
?- pubguide.

The following options are available :

To find which pubs are in each area of Anytown 1
To find which pubs have certain amenities  2
To find the amenities available at a given pub 3

Enter option 1 , 2 or 3

|: 1.
```

```
Areas of Anytown

town_centre   1
warwick_road  2
paddock_lane  3

Type in a number to choose a particular area

|:2.

List of pubs in warwick_road area

kings_head
sailors_rest
four_pennies
no
```

11.3 The travelling salesman problem

11.3.1 The problem

A travelling salesman has been given responsibility for sales within an area which covers 5 major towns. His work may involve travelling to any town within his territory at very short notice, in order to complete an important sale. Having done so, he may then be called upon to travel to any of the remaining towns within his area.

The salesman requires a system which will compute all of the possible routes between any two towns within his territory, along with the distance of each of these routes. This will enable him to:

plan routes which cover more than two towns , if need be

choose routes which use particular roads with which he is familiar

choose the shortest (i.e. cheapest) route.

The salesman's territory is depicted in Figure 11.1. The lines between the towns represent major roads and the distance between adjacent towns via these major roads is also marked on the diagram. If there is no line between two towns on the map, this means that there is no major road between these two towns.

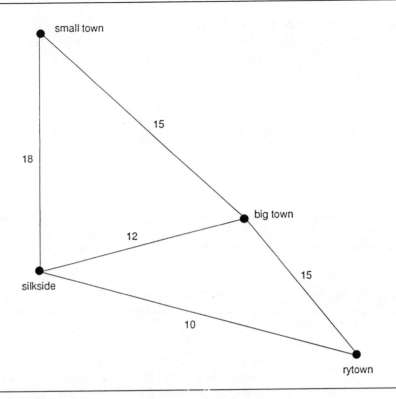

Fig. 11.1

11.3.2 Full program listing

```
/* travelling salesman program:/

run :-nl,nl,
      write(' Travelling salesman program'),
      nl,nl,nl,
      write('Type in first town').
      nl,
      read(Town1),
      nl,nl,
      write('Type in second town'),
      nl,
      read(Town2),
      route(Town1,Town2,[Town1],Way,Dist),
      nl,nl,
      write('One route from '),
      write(Town1),write(' to '),
```

```prolog
        write(Town2),write(' is : '),nl,
        write(Way),nl,nl,
        write('The distance is '),
        write(Dist),nl,nl,
        write('Do you wish to find another route ?'),nl,
        write('Answer yes or no '),nl,
        read(Response),
        act_on(Response).
```

/* the run predicate is the highest-level predicate
   which controls the operation of the program */

```prolog
act_on(yes) - nl,fail.
act_on(no).
```

/* act_on will cause backtracking (to locate other routes)
   if the user has typed yes . If the user has typed no
   the program will halt */

```prolog
route(Town,Town,_:Town],0)  :- !.

route(Town1,Town2,Covered,[Town1|:y],Dist)  :-
            go(Town1,Town3,Dist1),
            not(member(Town3,Covered)),
            route(Town3,Town2,[Town3|Covered],Way,Dist2),
            Dist is Dist1 + Dist2.
```

/* route(Town1,Town2,Covered,Way,Dist) succeeds if
   there is a route from Town1 to Town2 , Covered
   is a list of the towns covered so far, Way is a
   list containing the towns on the route and Dist
   is the distance covered by that route */

```prolog
member(X, [X|,_]).
member(X, [_|Y])  :- member(X,Y).

go(smalltown,bigtown15).
go(bigtown,smalltown,15).
go(smalltown,silkside,18).
go(silkside,smalltown,18).
go(bigtown,silkside,12).
go(silkside,bigtown,12).
go(silkside,rytown,10).
go(rytown,silkside,10).
go(bigtown,rytown,15).
go(rytown,bigtown,15).
```

```
/* go(X,Y,D) succeeds if you can go from town X
   to town Y and the distance between the two
   towns is D */
```

11.3.3 Notes

The travelling salesman program demonstrates Prolog's recursive problem solving capabilities. Prolog is often used to solve problems of this form (i.e. those which involve searching maps or mazes).

The main driving force of the program is the route predicate which is quite complex and hence requires a little further explanation.

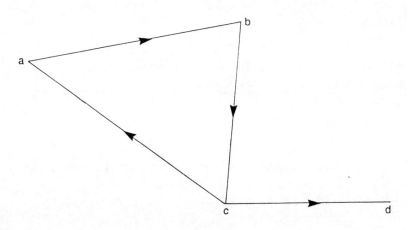

Fig. 11.2

It is probably easier if we first consider a simpler form of the program which can be used to search the map in Figure 11.2. This simplified program is given below.

```
/* simplified route program */

route(A,A).
route(A,B)  :- go(A,C),
               route(C,A).

go(a,b).
go(b,c).
go(c,a).
go(c,d).
```

The goal go(X,Y) succeeds if it is possible to travel from point X to point Y on the map. Notice that the roads on the simple map in Figure 11.2 are directional, that is they can only be traversed in one direction (as indicated by the arrows on the map). Thus the fact go(a,b) exists but the fact go(b,a) does not. In the full travelling salesman program above the roads can be traversed in either direction (so two go facts exist for each road).

The goal route(A,B) succeeds if there is a route from point A to point B on the map. The route predicate operates recursively in the following manner :

A route exists between point A and point B if you can go from point A to a point C and a route (which will be found recursively) exists from point C to point B.

The stopping condition route(A,A). comes into play when an attempt is made to travel from one point to itself.

For instance, the query

```
?- route(a,c).
```

will reduce to the conjunction of subgoals

```
go(a,b),
route(b,c).
```

The second of these subgoals will then result in the formation of the two subgoals

```
go(b,c),
route(c,c).
```

where route(c,C) will match with the stopping condition, causing the program to halt and provide the response yes.

There are several problems with this simple version of the route predicate :

First, there is nothing to prevent the program from looping indefinitely around any loops in the map. (A loop is a closed circular path - for example the points a , b and c form a loop.For instance, if we ask the program to find a route from a to d it will (because of the order in which the go facts are placed) find the route

a to b to c to a to b to c to a to b to c to a to ....

which will never stop!

Second, the program does not keep any record of the actual route covered. It simply informs the user whether or not there is a route (i.e. it answers yes or no!).

The route predicate in the full travelling salesman program has been designed to overcome the above two shortcomings. This is achieved in the following manner :

First, it records the towns already visited in a list called Covered. It then checks to ensure that any new town to be visited is not a member of Covered.

Second, it records the actual route covered and stores it in a list Way. Each time a town is visited it is added to the head of the list Way.

The above discussion explains the role of four of the five arguments of the route predicate in the full program. The fifth argument is Dist which simply computes the distance covered by the route.

It should be noted that this is a simple prototype system and represents a very small map. The program could easily be extended to cover larger maps by adding the necessary go facts. Be careful, however. Large maps may take an extremely long time to search!

11.3.4 Sample terminal session

```
?- run

Travelling Salesman Program


Type in first town
|:silkside.

Type in second town
|: rytown.

One route from silkside to rytown is :
[silkside,rytown]

The distance is 10

Do you wish to find another route?
Answer yes or no
|:yes.

One route from silkside to rytown is :
[silkside,smalltown,bigtown,rytown]
```

```
The distance is 48

Do you wish to find another route?
Answer yes or no
|: yes.

One route from silkside to rytown is :
[silkside,bigtown,rytown]

The distance is 27

Do you wish to find another route?
Answer yes or no
|: yes.

no
```

11.4 The periodic table

11.4.1 The problem

The periodic table lists all of the elements known to chemists. An element is a substance which cannot be broken down any further. The elements are listed in order according to their atomic numbers (for the technically-minded reader the atomic number of an element is equal to the number of electrons present in one atom of the element).

Each of the elements in the periodic table has several properties, some of the most important of which are:

atomic number (as outlined above)

the name of the element

a symbolic (shorthand) name for the element

the mass (i.e. atomic weight) of the element

The problem is to devise an expert system which embodies the above data for each element in the periodic table. The user should be able to:

type in the atomic number of an element and retrieve the corresponding data

type in the name of an element and retrieve the corresponding data.

11.4.2 The program listing

```
/* periodic table program */

table:- nl,nl,
        write('This program can provide you with'),nl,
        write('data from the periodic table'),
        nl,nl,nl,
        write('You can choose from two possible options'),
        nl,nl,
        write('To obtain data by atomic number
        type 1'),nl,
        write('To obtain data by element name type 2'),
        nl,nl,
        read(Numb),
        option(Numb).
```

/* table is the highest level predicate and controls
   the operation of the program. It presents the user
   with two possible choices,reads his response,and
   then passes control to the predicate option */

```
option(1):- nl,nl,
            write('Type in atomic number'),
            nl,nl,
            read(Atomic),
            nl,nl,
            element(Atomic,Name,Symbol,Mass),
            write('Name is  '),write(Name),nl,
            write('Symbol is '),write(Symbol),nl,
            write('Mass is  '),write(Mass),nl.
```

/* the first version of the option predicate allows the
   user to type in an atomic number and retrieve the
   data about the corresponding element */

```
option(2):- nl,nl,
            write('Type in an element name in lower
            case'),
            nl,nl,
            read(Name),
            nl,nl,
            element(Atomic,Name,Symbol,Mass),
            write('Atomic number is '),write(Atomic),nl,
            write('Symbol is'),write(Symbol),nl,
```

```
write('Mass is '),write(Mass),nl.
```

/* the second version of the option predicate allows the
   user to type in an element name and retrieve data about
   that element */

```
element(1,hydrogen,'H',1.0079).
element(2,helium,'He',4.0026).
element(3,lithium,'Li',6.941).
element(4,beryllium,'Be',9.0122).
element(5,boron,'B',10.81).
        .
        .
        .
etc.
        .
        .
```

/* the element(Atomic_number,Name,Symbol,Mass) facts
contain the data about the elements in the periodic table
*/

11.4.3 Notes

This is a relatively simple example of a Prolog system which is heavily "fact-based". Although only five element facts are listed above the complete system would comprise over one hundred facts as there are over one hundred currently known elements.

The operation of the program is straightforward and requires no further explanation. It relies solely on Prolog's pattern matching facilities to search through the database and find an appropriate match. It is really using Prolog as a form of database system and has no real intelligence. Such a system would take a remarkably short time to design and implement.

11.4.4 Sample terminal session

```
?- table.

This program can provide you with
data from the periodic table

You can choose from two possible options

To obtain data by atomic number type 1
```

```
To obtain data by element name type 2

|: 1.

Type in atomic number

|: 3.

Name is   lithium
Symbol is Li
Mass is   6.941
yes

?- table.

This program can provide you with
data from the periodic table

You can choose from two possible options

To obtain data by atomic number type 1
To obtain data by element name type 2

|: 2.

Type in element name in lower case

|: hydrogen.

Atomic number is 1
Symbol is H
Mass is 1.0079

yes
```

11.5 A program design aid

11.5.1 The problem

In order to understand this case study it is first necessary to briefly discuss some aspects of the program design process.

There are currently a large number of formal methods and "software tools" available to aid the programmer in the task of developing his software. These methods have, in particular, been applied to the development of data processing software; which is usually written in such procedural languages as COBOL.

A formal method is a set of rules which, if followed correctly, will guarantee that the programmer will produce a correct and well structured program.

A software tool is a program which is designed to help the programmer to design his program, often according to the rules of the particular formal method which he is following.

This case study is concerned with a software tool which is designed to help programmers to test their software. It is designed for use by programmers who are employing one particular formal method; namely Jackson Structured Programming (JSP). The program described in this section forms one small part of a much larger software tool which has been developed by the author in conjunction with Mr. R.M.F Roper of Sunderland Polytechnic.

Jackson Structured Programming (JSP) is a formal method which is commonly applied in the production of data processing programs. It is beyond the scope of this text to attempt to describe the full method. However, it is necessary to outline one particular feature of the method so that the reader can understand the operation of the Prolog program described in this case study.

One important aspect of JSP involves representing a program by means of a "structure chart". A structure chart is a diagrammatic means of expressing the structure of a program in terms of three basic constructs

sequence

selection

iteration

The diagrammatic forms of these constructs are depicted in Figures 11.3, 11.4 and 11.5, along with descriptions of their meanings. A full structure chart is depicted in Figure 11.6. It can be seen that this chart is comprised solely of sequences, selections and iterations. A single box in the chart which does not have any boxes below it (i.e. child components) is known as an elementary box.

The problem is to create a software tool which will allow a programmer to enter a JSP structure chart and store it as a series of Prolog facts. Once the chart has been stored as a series of Prolog facts other tools can then be used to perform further manipulations on it.

This tool forms the initial part of a much larger tool (not described here) which then goes on to produce tests which the programmer can use to ensure, as far as possible, that his program is functioning correctly. (For any reader interested in seeing a listing of the full Prolog tool a reference to this work is included in the bibliography).

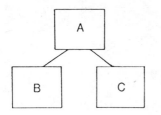

The sequence A consists of performing B followed by C.

Fig. 11.3

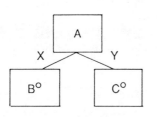

The selection A consists of performing EITHER B OR C (depending on conditions X and Y).

i.e. If X is true then perform B else if Y is true perform C.

Fig. 11.4

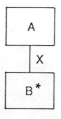

The iteration A consists of performing B a certain number of times (according to the condition X)

Fig 11.5

11.5.2 Full program listing

```
/* program to input a JSP chart */

input_tree:- write('number of boxes in chart? '),
             read(N),
             input_nodes(N).
```

```
/* input routine - reads from the terminal the number of
boxes in a chart and calls input_nodes */
```

```
input_nodes(0):- !.
```

```
input_nodes(N):- write('name of node ?'),
                 read(Name),
                 write('type of construct?'),
                 read(Type),
                 add_fact(Type,Name),
                 M is N - 1,
                 input_nodes(M).
```

/* reads a component and adds a corresponding fact
to the knowledge base */

```
add_fact(sequence,Name):- write('number of child
                                 components?'),
                          read(Num),
                          input_comp(Num,List_comp),
                          assertz(sequence(Name,
                                  List_comp)).
```

/* collects the attributes of a sequence
  (i.e. the number and names of children)
  and makes an assertion with this information */

```
input_comp(0,[]):- !.

input_comp(N:,[Comp_name|L1]):- write('name of child
                                       component?'),
                                read(Comp_name),
                                M is N - 1,
                                input_comp(M,L1).
```

/* inputs a list of child components */

```
add_fact(iteration,Name):- write('condition?'),
                           read(Condition),
                           write('name of child
                                 component?'),
                           read(Comp_name),
                           assertz(iteration(Name,
                                   Condition,Comp_name)).
```

/* asserts an iteration and its attributes
  i.e. name, condition and name of child */

```
add_fact(selection,Name):- write('number of child
                                  components?'),
                           read(Num),
```

```
                    input_cond(Num,List_cond),
                    input_comp(Num,List_comp),
                    assertz(selection(Name,
                    List_cond, List_comp)).
```

/* asserts a selection with name, a list of conditions
   and a list of child components controlled by those
   conditions */

```
input_cond(0,[]):- !.

input_cond(:m,[Cond_name|L1]):- write('condition?'),
                                read(Cond_name),
                                M is Num - 1,
                                input_ cond(M,L1).
```

/* inputs a list of conditions */

```
add_fact(elementary,Name):- assertz(elementary(Name)).
```

/* asserts an elementary component */

11.5.3 Notes

This case study illustrates two important points:

> it demonstrates the important role which Prolog has to play in the
> development of "intelligent" software tools.

> it serves as an example of a Prolog system which can "learn" from the user's
> responses to its questions. That is, the program creates its own knowledge
> base as the program runs.

The program in the previous section is well-commented and should, therefore, be self-
explanatory. The terminal session below demonstrates its operation.

11.5.4 Sample terminal session

Note: the structure chart on which this terminal session is based is depicted in Figure
11.6.

```
        ?- input_tree.
        number of boxes in chart? |: 9.
```

```
name of node? |: top.
type of construct? |: sequence.
number of child components? |: 3.
name of child component? |: a.
name of child component? |: b.
name of child component? |: c.
name of node? |: a.
type of construct? |: selection.
number of child components? |: 2.
condition? |: x.
condition? |: y.
name of child component? |: d.
name of child component? |: e.
name of node? |: b.
type of construct? |: iteration.
condition? |: z.
name of child component? |: f.
name of node? |: c.
type of construct? |: sequence.
number of child components? |: 2.
name of child component? |: g.
name of child component? |: h.
name of node? |: d.
type of construct? |: elementary.
name of node? |: e.
type of construct? |: elementary.
name of node? |: f.
type of construct? |: elementary.
name of node? |: g.
type of construct? |: elementary.
name of node? |: h.
type of construct? |: elementary.
yes

?- listing(sequence).
sequence(top, [a, b, c]).
sequence(c, [g, h]).

?- listing(selection).
selection(a, [x, y], [d, e]).

?- listing(iteration).
iteration(b, z, f).

?- listing(elementary).
elementary(d).
```

184

```
elementary(e).
elementary(f).
elementary(g).
elementary(h).
```

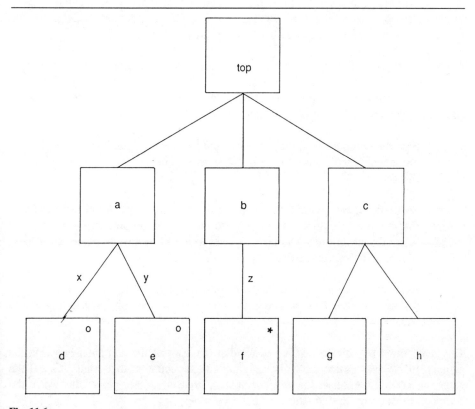

Fig. 11.6

11.6 A noughts and crosses game

11.6.1 The problem

The powerful facilities and features of Prolog make it an ideal language in which to implement games programs, particularly those which involve the use of rules. This case study considers the development of one such program, namely a noughts and crosses game.

The idea behind this noughts and crosses program is that the game will involve a contest between a human (the user) and the computer.The user will be free to choose his own moves while the computer will also choose where to make its moves, based on its own "intelligence", which will be built into the program in the form of Prolog rules.

The user will play crosses while the computer will play noughts. The game will display the noughts and crosses 'board' on the screen after each move is made, thus giving the user a clear picture of the current state of play of the game.

The user starts the game by making an initial move and placing a cross on the board. The computer will then respond by placing a nought on the board. The program will have sufficient intelligence built into it to enable the computer to use the following logic when deciding where to place its nought on the board:

> First the computer will play to win at the next move. That is, it will look for a move which will cause it to win the game. If such a move exists, it will make that move.

> Secondly, if the computer cannot win at the next move, it will try to ensure that the user does not win. In order to do so, the computer will look for any move that it is forced to make in order to avoid losing the game at the next move. If such a move exists, it will make that move.

> Finally, if the computer cannot win at the next move, and it is not necessary to prevent the user from winning, the computer will simply play in any empty square.

The game must be able to detect when either the user or the computer has won the game, print an appropriate error message and halt the game at that point. Also, if the game has come to an unsatisfactory conclusion, (that is, neither player has won), the computer must detect this situation and act accordingly.

Finally, it goes without saying that the game must be designed to be as easy-to-play as possible. A games program which is difficult to play is something of a contradiction in terms!

11.6.2 Full program listing

```
/* a noughts and crosses game */

game :- initialise,
        user_play(b(A,B,C,D,E,F,G,H,I)).

/* game is the top-level predicate which starts the
game */
```

```prolog
initialise :- nl,nl,
       write('Program to play noughts and crosses'),
       nl,nl,
       write('The computer will play noughts
       and'),nl,
       write('you will play crosses'),nl,nl,
       write('You will be prompted to enter'),
       write(' your move '),nl,
       write('according to the numbers shown in
       the'),write(' board below :'),nl,nl,
       write_board(b(1,2,3,4,5,6,7,8,9)),nl,nl,
       write('The game will now begin'),nl,nl,
       write('**********************************
       ******'),nl,nl,nl.
```

/* initialise prints an initial explanation of the
game */
```prolog
user_play(Board) :- user_input(Board),
       write_board(Board),
       check_state(Board,user).
```

/* user_play makes a move for the user */

```prolog
computer_play(Board) :- check_finish(Board).
```

/* this version of computer_play checks whether
  or not the game is finished */

```prolog
computer_play(Board) :- nl,
               write('Now it''s my turn to play !'),nl,
               choose_move(Board),
               write_board(Board),
               check_state(Board,computer).
```

/* this version of computer_play will make a move
for the computer */

```prolog
check_finish(Board) :- check_square(8,Board),nl,
       write('Game over. '),
       write('No winner this time ! '),nl,nl.
```

/* check_finish terminates the program */

```prolog
check_square(1,Board) :- arg(1,Board,X),nonvar(X).
check_square(N,Board) :- arg(N,Board,X),nonvar(X),
                         M is N - 1,
```

```
        check_square(M,Board).

/* check_square is used to check if the board is
full */
check_state(Board,Player) :- win(Board,Player),
        message(Player).
check_state(Board,user) :- computer_play(Board).
check_state(Board,computer) :- user_play(Board).

/* check_state is used to check the state of the
game to see whose turn it is to play and whether the
game has been won */

message(user) :- nl,nl,
        write('You have won !!!!!'),nl,nl,
        write('Well done !!!!'),nl,nl.

message(computer) :- nl,nl,
write('I have won !!!!!'), nl,nl,
        write('Better luck next time !!!!'),nl,nl.

/* message writes out an appropriate winning message
*/

win(Board,Player) :- line(Squares),
        winner(Squares,Board,Player).

/* win checks for a win */

winner([X,Y,Z],Board,user) :- cross(X,Board),
        cross(Y,Board),
        cross(Z,Board).

winner([X,Y,Z],Board,computer) :- nought(X,Board),
        nought(Y,Board),
        nought(Z,Board).

/* winner is used to check a win for a particular
player */

user_input(Board) :- nl,nl,
        write('Move required ?'),
        read(Sq),
        arg(Sq,Board,Val),
        var(Val),
        arg(Sq,Board,x).
```

```
/* user_input accepts the user's move */

choose_move(Board) :- win_move(Board,Sq),
 arg(Sq,Board,o).

choose_move(Board) :- must_play(Board,Sq),
 arg(Sq,Board,o).
choose_move(Board) :- play_any(Board,Sq),
 arg(Sq,Board,o).

/* choose_move is used by the computer to choose a
move according to the following strategy :
  - first look for a winning move
  - then, if you cannot win, prevent the user from
    winning on his next move if necessary
  - else play any move */

win_move(Board,Sq) :- line(Squares),
      win_line(Squares,Board,Sq).

/* win_move chooses a winning move by looking for
  a possible winning line */

win_line([X,Y,Z],Board,X) :- empty(X,Board),
      nought(Y,Board),
      nought(Z,Board).

win_line([X,Y,Z],Board,Y) :- empty(Y,Board),
      nought(X,Board),
      nought(Z,Board).

win_line([X,Y,Z],Board,Z) :- empty(Z,Board),
      nought(X,Board),
      nought(Y,Board).

/* win_line searches for a winning line */

must_play(Board,Sq) :- line(Squares),
      threat(Squares,Board,Sq).

/* must_play searches for any moves which the
computer must make in order to avoid losing at the
next move  - this is done by searching for lines
which represent a threat i.e. will cause the user to
win on his next move */
```

```prolog
threat([X,Y,Z],Board,X) :- empty(X,Board),
      cross(Y,Board),
      cross(Z,Board).

threat([X,Y,Z],Board,Y) :- empty(Y,Board),
      cross(X,Board),
      cross(Z,Board).

threat([X,Y,Z],Board,Z) :- empty(Z,Board),
      cross(X,Board),
      cross(Y,Board).
```

/* threat searches for lines which are a threat
   (as defined above)   */

```prolog
play_any(Board,Sq) :- square(Sq),
      arg(Sq,Board,Val),
      var(Val).
```

/* play_any will play any move, simply by choosing
   the first free square (in numeric order) */

```prolog
square(1).
square(X) :- square(Y),
      X is Y + 1,
      X > 0,
      X < 10.
```

/* square chooses a free square */

```prolog
write_board(Board) :- nl,write_line(1,Board),nl,
      write('_____'),nl,
      write_line(4,Board),nl,
      write('_____'),nl,
      write_line(7,Board),nl,nl.
```

/* write_board writes the board */

```prolog
write_line(X,Board) :- arg(X,Board,V1),tab(1),
      write_sq(V1),
      tab(1),write('I'),tab(1),
      Y is X + 1,
      arg(Y,Board,V2),
      write_sq(V2),
      tab(1),write('I'),tab(1),
```

```
          Z is Y + 1,
          arg(Z,Board,V3),
          write_sq(V3).

   /* write_line writes one line of the board */

   write_sq(X)  :- var(X),tab(1).

   write_sq(X)  :- nonvar(X),write(X).

   /* write_sq writes one square of the board */
   line([1,2,3]).
   line([4,5,6]).
   line([7,8,9]).
   line([1,4,7]).
   line([2,5,8]).
   line([3,6,9]).
   line([1,5,9]).
   line([3,5,7]).

   /* the line facts contain all of the valid lines */

   empty(Sq,Board)  :- arg(Sq,Board,Val),var(Val).

   /* empty is used to check for an empty square */

   cross(Sq,Board)  :- arg(Sq,Board,Val), nonvar(Val),
          Val = x.

   /* cross is used to check for a square occupied by a
   cross */

   nought(Sq,Board)  :- arg(Sq,Board,Val),
   nonvar(Val),
   Val = o.

   /* nought is used to check for a square occupied by
   a cross */
```

11.6.3 Notes

As you will have seen, the Prolog code for the noughts and crosses game is quite lengthy and it would take a good deal of explanation to discuss the operation of every predicate in detail. The comments within the program should be sufficient to enable the reader to understand the way in which the program implements the game and the sample terminal session in the following section of this chapter will also serve in that capacity.

It should, however, be noted that the noughts and crosses board:

```
    I    I
   _____
    I    I
   _____
    I    I
```

is represented by the Prolog structure

b(A,B,C,D,E,F,G,H,I)

where the variables A,B,C,D,E,F,G,H and I can have one of three possible values:

uninstantiated (to represent an empty square),

o (to represent a nought), and

x (to represent a cross).

The board below:

```
   o I x I x
  _____
   o I x I
  _____
   o I o I x
```

would, therefore, be represented by the following structure:

b(o,x,x,o,x,F,o,o,x) .

It should also be noted that the intelligence which the computer uses to make its move is somewhat limited, to say the least. In particular, the play_any predicate (which causes the computer to make a "random" move) could be replaced by a series of rules to enable the computer to choose its move more carefully, and on a more sensible basis. For instance, the program could be extended to include rules which would look for a win in two moves' time, rather than simply looking one move ahead as is the case in the current version of the game. It is left to the reader to extend the game in such a manner, if he so desires.

11.6.4 Sample terminal session

The terminal session below includes an example of each of the three possible outcomes of a noughts and crosses game; namely:

> the user wins
> the computer wins
> neither player wins

In the examples, the initial dialogue is only shown for the first session:

Example 1

```
?- game.

Program to play noughts and crosses
The computer will play noughts and
you will play crosses
You will be prompted to enter your move
according to the numbers shown in the board below:

 1 I 2 I 3
_____
 4 I 5 I 6
_____
 7 I 8 I 9

The game will now begin

****************************************

Move required ? 1.

 x I   I
_____
   I   I
_____
   I   I

Now it's my turn to play !

 x I o I
_____
   I   I
_____
   I   I
```

Move required ? 5.

```
 x I o I
_____
   I x I
_____
   I   I
```

Now it's my turn to play !

```
 x I o I
_____
   I x I
_____
   I   I o
```

Move required ? 7.

```
 x I o I
_____
   I x I
_____
 x I   I o
```

Now it's my turn to play !

```
 x I o I
_____
 o I x I
_____
 x I   I o
```

Move required ? 3.

```
 x I o I x
_____
 o I x I
_____
 x I   I o
```

You have won !!!!!

Well done !!!!

Example 2

Move required ? 2.

```
  I x I
_____
  I   I
_____
  I   I
```

Now it's my turn to play !

```
o I x I
_____
  I   I
_____
  I   I
```

Move required ? 5.

```
o I x I
_____
  I x I
_____
  I   I
```

Now it's my turn to play !

```
o I x I
_____
  I x I
_____
  I o I
```

Move required ? 3.

```
o I x I x
_____
  I x I
_____
  I o I
```

Now it's my turn to play !

```
  o I x I x
_____
  I x I
_____
  o I o I
```

Move required ? 9.

```
  o I x I x
_____
  I x I
_____
  o I o I x
```

Now it's my turn to play !

```
  o I x I x
_____
  o I x I
_____
  o I o I x
```

I have won !!!!!

Better luck next time !!!!

Example 3

Move required ? 5.

```
  I   I
_____
  I x I
_____
  I   I
```

Now it's my turn to play !

```
  o I   I
_____
  I x I
_____
  I   I
```

Move required ? 3.

```
o I   I x
─────────
  I x I
─────────
  I   I
```

Now it's my turn to play !

```
o I   I x
─────────
  I x I
─────────
o I   I
```

Move required ? 4.

```
o I   I x
─────────
x I x I
─────────
o I   I
```

Now it's my turn to play !

```
o I   I x
─────────
x I x I o
─────────
o I   I
```

Move required ? 2.

```
o I x I x
─────────
x I x I o
─────────
o I   I
```

Now it's my turn to play !

```
o I x I x
─────────
x I x I o
─────────
o I o I
```

```
Move required ? 9.

   o I x I x
   _____
   x I x I o
   _____
   o I o I x
```

Game over. No winner this time !

11.7 Symbolic differentiation

11.7.1 The problem

This case study is designed to demonstrate the ability of Prolog to manipulate symbols. In this particular instance we are utilising the symbolic manipulation properties of Prolog in the development of an expert system which can perform symbolic differentiation. A commercially available expert system named MACSYMA, which has very powerful features for performing integration, differentiation, and general equation solving is based upon these principles.

The objective of this case study is to develop a system which can implement some of the basic rules of differentiation. The rules in question are:

$$dx/dx = 1$$
$$dc/dx = 0 \qquad \text{where c is a constant}$$
$$d(u+v)/dx = du/dx + dv/dx$$
$$d(u-v)/dx = du/dx - dv/dx$$
$$d(c*u)/dx = c*du/dx$$
$$d(u*v)/dx = u*dv/dx + v*du/dx \text{ (the product rule)}$$
$$d(u/v)/dx = (v*du/dx - u*dv/dx)/v^2 \text{ (the quotient rule)}$$

The system should enable the user to type in an algebraic expression and then ask him with respect to which variable he wishes to differentiate. The system should then produce the derivative of that expression in as simple a form as possible.

11.7.2 Full program listing

```
/* program to perform symbolic differentiation */

maths:- nl,nl,
    write('This program will differentiate'),nl,
    write('mathematical functions for you '),nl,nl,
    write('Type in the function to be'),
```

```
        write(' differentiated '),nl,
        read(Function),nl,
        write('Differentiate with respect to ?'),nl,
        read(Wrt),nl,
        diff(Function,Wrt,Result),
        write('Level of simplification required ?'),nl,
        write('- lowest level is 0 for no '),
        write('simplification'),nl,
        write('- there is no upper limit '),nl,
        read(Numb),nl,nl,
        simp(Result,Simp,Numb),
        write('The differential is : '),nl,nl,
        write(Simp),nl,nl.

/* diff is the top level predicate and controls
   the operation of the program */

diff(X,X,1).

/* the derivative of x is x */

diff(C,X,0) :- atomic(C).

/* the derivative of a constant is 0 */

diff(U + V,X,A + B) :- diff(U,X,A),
                       diff(V,X,B).

/* the derivative of the sum of two functions
   Is the sum of their derivatives */

diff(U - V,X,A - B) :- diff(U,X,A),
                       diff(V,X,B).

/* the derivative of the difference of two functions
is the difference of their derivatives */

diff(C * U,X,C * A) :- atomic(C),
                       C \= X,
                       diff(X,A).

/* the derivative of a constant times a function
   is the constant times the derivative of the
   function */

diff(U * V,X,B * U + A * V) :- diff(U,X,A),
```

```
        diff(V,X,B).

/* the 'product' rule */

diff(U / V,X,V * A / V * V - U * B / V * V )  :-
        diff(U,X,A),
        diff(V,X,B).

/* the quotient rule */

simp(X,X,0)  :- !.
simp(Expr,Result,N)  :- M is N - 1,
        simplify(Expr,Res1),
        simp(Res1,Result,M).

/* simp will make the number of simplifications
   requested by the user */

simplify(X * 0,0).
simplify(0 + X,0).
simplify(0 + X,0).
simplify(X + 0,X).
simplify(X - 0,X).
simplify(X * 1,X).
simplify(1 * X,X).

simplify(A * X + B * X,C * X)  :- integer(A),
                                  integer(B),
                                  C is A + B.
simplify(A,A).
/* algebraic simplification rules */
```

11.7.3 Notes

The diff clauses in the above program are almost a straight translation from the mathematical formulae listed in Section 11.7.1. The operation of the full program is as follows:

> the user is asked to type in an expression, the variable with respect to which the differentiation is to take place, and the 'level of simplification' required

> the program then uses the predicate diff to apply the rules of differentiation to the expression - these rules are applied recursively where necessary

> the program then uses the predicate simp to simplify the expression to the required level

> finally, the simplified expression is written out to the terminal

The idea of 'level of simplification' has been introduced to enable the user to simplify the expression to the greatest possible level. For example, a level of simplification of 0 (which is, in fact, equivalent to no simplification at all) might result in the line

```
1*x+1*x+0
```

being output. Simplifying this expression one level further (i.e. level = 1) would produce the result

```
1*x+1*x
```

while a further simplification would produce

```
2*x
```

Any further simplifications would, obviously, be a waste of time at this stage as this expression is already now in its simplest form.

As the level of simplification required will vary, depending upon the complexity of the expression to be simplified, the program leaves it up to the user to choose the level to employ. It should, however, be stated that the rules of simplification (i.e. the simplify clauses) are very restricted and, for this reason, there are some expressions which can not be simplified to their greatest extent. The terminal session in the next section illustrates the role of simplification in the program.

11.7.4 Sample terminal session

Example 1

```
Type in the function to be differentiated
x*x-4*x+6.

Differentiate with respect to ?
x.

Level of simplification required ?
- lowest level is 0 for no simplification
- there is no upper limit
0.

The differential is:
1*x+1*x-(1*4+0*x)+0
```

Some additional examples are shown on the next page:

Example 2

```
Type in the function to be differentiated
x*x-4*x+6.

Differentiate with respect to ?
x.

Level of simplification required ?
- lowest level is 0 for no simplification
- there is no upper limit
3.

The differential is:

1*x+1*x-(1*4+0*x)
```

Example 3

```
Type in the function to be differentiated
x*x+5*x*x.

Differentiate with respect to ?
x.

Level of simplification required ?
- lowest level is 0 for no simplification
- there is no upper limit
2.
The differential is:
1*x+1*x+(1*(5*x)+(1*5+0*x)*x)
```

Example 4

```
Type in the function to be differentiated
x*x*x-4*x*x+23*x-99.

Differentiate with respect to ?
x.

Level of simplification required ?
- lowest level is 0 for no simplification
- there is no upper limit
4.
The differential is:
1*(x*x)+(1*x+1*x)*x-(1*(4*x)+(1*4+0*x)*x)+(1*23+0*x)
```

11.8 The towers of Hanoi (in Turbo Prolog)

11.8.1 The Problem

The final case study is implemented in Turbo Prolog to provide a further example of that particular version of the language.

Prolog is also extremely well suited to the solution of problems in general. That is, if the solution to a problem can be written in a general form it is often quite straightforward to translate that solution into Prolog. The resultant program can then be used to solve the problem for any particular instance.

The Towers of Hanoi problem is a well known puzzle which many readers may have seen as a children's toy. The puzzle consists of a collection of wooden (or plastic) discs and three upright poles onto which the discs can be slotted. The discs are all of decreasing size and are initially all slotted on the left pole as shown in Figure 11.7.

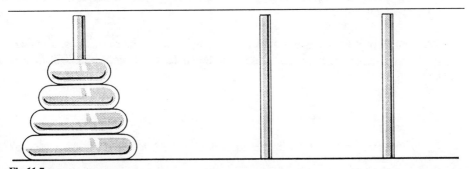

Fig 11.7

The object of the exercise is to move all of the discs from the left pole to the right pole. The player must, however, observe the following rules:

> only one disc may be moved at a time

> a larger disc may not be placed on top of a smaller disc

The middle pole may, of course, be used as a "spare" on which to rest discs during the course of moving the discs.

If you have ever been presented with such a puzzle you will soon realise that, although it may be easy to solve the puzzle for a small number of discs (say, one, two or three), it is by no means a simple feat to solve it for a large number of discs.

A solution can, however, be stated in the following general terms:

moving N discs from the left pole to the right pole consists of:

> moving N - 1 discs from the left pole to the middle pole
> moving the remaining (bottom and largest) disc from the left pole to the right pole
> moving the N - 1 discs from the middle pole to the right pole

As you will have noticed, the first and the last of the three stages outlined above are stated in very general terms and, at first sight, may appear to be of little practical use. That is, the exercise of moving N - 1 discs from one pole to another cannot be achieved simply by picking up the whole pile of N - 1 discs and relocating them all in a single move. Such a move would surely break the rules of the game! However, the general solution stated above can be applied in a recursive fashion to the problem of moving N - 1 discs.

It is the recursive nature of the general solution above which makes it an ideal candidate for a Prolog program. The program shown below is, therefore, based upon a recursive predicate move.

The program allows the user to request a solution for any number of discs. The exact moves required to move those discs from the left pole to the right pole will then be displayed on the screen.

11.8.2 Full program listing

```
/* towers of hanoi program in Turbo Prolog */

domains
        pole = right ; left ; middle

predicates
        hanoi(integer)
        move(integer,pole,pole,pole)
        write_message(pole,pole)

clauses

  hanoi(N) if move(N,left,middle,right) and
          write("\nFinished \n").
  /* hanoi is the top level goal which succeeds
     by moving N discs from the left pole to the
        right pole using the middle pole as a spare */

  move(0,_,_,_) if !.
  move(N,A,B,C) if M = N - 1 and
          move(M,A,C,B) and
```

```
          write_message(A,C) and
          move(M,B,A,C).
```

/* the recursive move predicate is the driving
   force of the program and implements the three-
   stage solution described in the previous section
   - the stopping condition is reached when the
   number of discs to be moved is zero */

```
write_message(A,B) if
write("\nMove a disc from ",A," to ",B).
```

/* the write_message predicate is used to
   display the moves made by the program
   and represents the movement of one disc
   from one pole to another */

11.8.3 Notes

The number of moves necessary to move the discs from the left pole to the right pole increases dramatically as the number of discs increases. Similarly, the depth of recursion (and hence the time taken to produce a solution) will increase as you increase the value of n in the goal hanoi(n). For this reason, the reader is advised to experiment with small values of n first. If you have a children's version of the puzzle it is, of course, quite easy (and fun!) to check that the moves which the program provides are actually correct.

11.8.4 Sample terminal session

```
Goal : hanoi(3).
Move a disc from left to right
Move a disc from left to middle
Move a disc from right to middle
Move a disc from left to right
Move a disc from middle to left
Move a disc from middle to right
Move a disc from left to right
Finished
Goal : hanoi(4).
Move a disc from left to middle
Move a disc from left to right
Move a disc from middle to right
Move a disc from left to middle
Move a disc from right to left
Move a disc from right to middle
```

```
Move a disc from left to middle
Move a disc from left to right
Move a disc from middle to right
Move a disc from middle to left
Move a disc from right to left
Move a disc from middle to right
Move a disc from left to middle
Move a disc from left to right
Move a disc from middle to right
Finished
```

SOLUTIONS TO SELECTED EXERCISES

Chapter 3.

1.   (a) `likes(tony,swimming).`

        (b) `is(rolls_royce,large_expensive_car).`

        (c) `chase(dogs,cats).`

        (d) `flies(alison,plane).`

        (e) `tall(harry).`

        (f) `friends(susan,terry,elaine,tracy).`

2.   `married(anthony,mary).`
        `married(trevor,hazel).`

        `male(anthony).`
        `male(harry).`
        `male(trevor).`
        `male(john).`

        `female(mary).`
        `female(claire).`
        `female(hazel).`

        `parents(harry,anthony,mary).`
        `parents(claire,anthony,mary).`
        `parents(hazel,anthony,mary).`
        `parents(john,trevor,hazel).`

(a)   `?- parents(harry,Pa,Ma),parents(X,Pa,Ma),female(X).`
(b)   `?- parents(hazel,Pa,Ma),parents(X,Ma,Pa),male(X).`
(c)   `?- parents(john,Pa,_).`
(d)   `?- parents(claire,_,Ma).`
(e)   `?- married(X,Y).`

Note. There are several other ways in which the knowledge base could have been structured. The queries would then, of course, also take on a different form.

Chapter 4.

2. (a)

```
interviewee(X)  :- drive(X),
                   lives(X,london).
                   type(X).
```

(b)

```
lives(john_smith,cambridge).
lives(charles_brown,london).
lives(mary_jones,glasgow).
lives(tony_evans,london).
lives(alice_green,luton).



drive(john_smith).
drive(charles_brown).
drive(tony_evans).
drive(alice_green).

type(charles_brown).
type(mary_jones).
type(tony_evans).
type(alice_green).
```

(c)

```
?- interviewee(X).
X = charles_brown ? ;
X = tony_evans ? ;
no
```

Chapter 5

1.

```
valid_trip(X)  :- timetable(X,Dist,Cost),
                  Dist =< 125,
                  Cost =< 20.

timetable(edinburgh,405,55).
timetable(brighton,53,12.5)
timetable(newcastle,278,39).
timetable(luton,32,14).
timetable(cambridge,60,18).
timetable(reading,40,8).
```

Chapter 6

2.
```
sum(0.0) :- 1.
sum(Int,Result) :- Int1 is Int - 1,
                   sum(Int1,Res1),
                   Result is Res1 + Int.
```

3.
```
average(Int,Result) :- sum(Int,Res1),
                       Int1 is Int + 1,
                       Result is Res1 / Int1.
```

5.
```
count(0,0) :- ! .
count(X,Y) :- M is X div 10,
              count(M,Z),
              Y is Z + 1.
```

6.
```
pol(0,X,1) :- !.
pol(1,X,X) :- !.
pol(N,X,R) :- M is N - 1,
              pol(M,X,Z),
              K is N - 2,
              pol(K,X,W),
              A is 2 * N - 1,
              B is A * X * Z - M * W,
              Y is B / N.
```

Chapter 7

1.(a)
```
subset([A|X]Y) :- member(A,Y)
                  subset(X,Y) .
subset([],Y) .
```

(b)
```
union([],X,X).
union([X|R],Y,Z) :- member(X,Y), !,
                    union(R,Y,Z) .
union([X|R],Y,[X|Z]) :- union(R,Y,Z) .
```

(c)

```
intersection([],X,[]).
intersection([X|R],Y,[X|Z]) :- member(X,Y), !,
                                 intersection(R,Y,Z).
intersection([X|R],Y,Z) :- intersection(R,Y,Z).
```

2.(a)

```
integers(High,High,[High]) :- !.
integers(Low,High,[Low|Rest]) :- M is Low + 1,
                                 integers(M,High,Rest).
```

(b)

```
remove(P,[],[]).
remove(P,[I|Is],[I|Nis]) :- not(0 is I mod P), !,
                            remove(P,Is,Nis).
remove(P,[I|Is],Nis) :- 0 is I mod P, !,
                        remove(P,Is,Nis).
```

(c)

```
sift([],[]).
sift([I|Is],[I|Primes]) :- remove(I,Is,New),
                           sift(New,Primes).
primes(Limit,Primes) :- integers(2,Limit,Is),
                        sift(Is,Primes).
```

Chapter 8

2.

```
run :- write('Type in an integer'),nl,
       read(X),
       Z is X * X,
       count(Z,Y),
       write('Number of digits in square is '),
       write(Y),nl.
```

The predicate count is defined in the solution to Exercise 5 in Chapter 6 (see above).

BIBLIOGRAPHY

A. General texts on expert systems, fifth generation systems and Artificial Intelligence

Alty J.L. and Coombs M.J., *Expert Systems - Concepts and examples*, NCC, 1984.

Bidmead C, *Food for thought*, Practical Computing,pp 128-130, Oct 1984.

Bird J, *Fifth Generation (Special report)*, Computing Europe, pp 19-28, 1982.

Bramer M and Bramer D, *The Fifth Generation - an annotated bibliography*, Addison-Wesley, 1984.

Brandin D.H, *The Challenge of the Fifth Generation*, Comms ACM, Vol 25, No 8, pp 509-510, 1982.

Brooking A, *Making computers more knowledgeable*, DEC User, pp 30-31, 33-34, Dec 1983.

Durham T, *Fifth Generation Fever*, Practical Computing, Oct 1984, pp 115,117.

Feigenbaum E.A and McCorduck P, *The Fifth Generation : Artificial Intelligence and Japan's Computer Challenge to the World*, Addison-Wesley 1983.

Fuchi K, *The direction the FGCS project will take*, New Generation Computing, Vol 1, No 1, pp 3-9, 1983.

Gondran M, *An Introduction to Expert Systems*, McGraw Hill, 1983.,

Hayes-Roth F, Wateman D.A and Lenat D.B (eds) , *Building Expert Systems*, Addison-Wesley, 1983.,

Jackson P, *Introduction to Expert Systems*, Addison-Wesley, 1986.,

Michaelsen R and Michie D, *Expert Systems in Business*, Datamation, Vol 29, No 4, pp 204-246, 1983.,

Michie D (ed), *Expert Systems in the Micro-Electronic Age*, Edinburgh University Press, 1979.,

Michie D (ed), *Introductory Readings in Expert Systems*, Gordon and Breach, 1982.,

Naughton J, *Products bring expertise to industry, military*, DEC User, pp 29 - 35, July 1982.,

Naughton J, *How to computerise an expert's knowledge*, DEC User, pp 51 - 55, Aug 1985.,

Rich E, *Artificial Intelligence*, McGraw Hill 1983.,

Simons G.L, *Towards Fifth Generation Computers*, NCC, 1983.,

Wellbank M, *A Review of Knowledge Acquisition Techniques for Expert Systems*, British Telecom, 1983.,

Winfield M.J, *Expert Systems : An introduction for the layman*, Computer Bulletin,pp 6,7,18, Dec 1982.,

Winston P.H, *Artificial Intelligence*, Addison-Wesley, 1984.,

B. Texts on Prolog programming and applications

Bratko I, *Prolog Programming and Artificial Intelligence*, Addison-Wesley, 1986.

Burnham W.D and Hall A.R, *Prolog Programming and Applications*, MacMillan, 1985.

Clocksin W.F and Mellish C.S, *Programming in Prolog*, Springer-Verlag, 1981.

Goodall A, *Logic Programming in Prolog*, Data Processing, Vol 26, No 2, pp 37-39,48, 1984.

Malpas J, *Prolog: A Relational language and its Applications*, Prentice-Hall, 1987.

Roper R.M.F and Smith P, *A Software Tool for Testing JSP Designed Programs*, Software Engineering Journal, Vol 2, No 2, pp 46-52, 1987.

ASCII Character Set

Char	Code	Char	Code
space	32	P	80
!	33	Q	81
"	34	R	82
#	35	S	83
$	36	T	84
%	37	U	85
&	38	V	86
'	39	W	87
(	40	X	88
)	41	Y	89
*	42	Z	90
+	43	[	91
,	44	\	92
-	45	]	93
.	46	^	94
/	47		95
0	48	`	96
1	49	a	97
2	50	b	98
3	51	c	99
4	52	d	100
5	53	e	101
6	54	f	102
7	55	g	103
8	56	h	104
9	57	i	105
:	58	j	106
;	59	k	107
<	60	l	108
=	61	m	109
>	62	n	110
?	63	o	111
@	64	p	112
A	65	q	113
B	66	r	114
C	67	s	115
D	68	t	116
E	69	u	117
F	70	v	118
G	71	w	119
H	72	x	120
I	73	y	121
J	74	z	122
K	75	{	123
L	76			124
M	77	}	125
N	78	~	126
O	79		

APPENDIX B

List of Operators

This appendix lists the operators which are covered in this book with typical values for Precedence and Associativity.

Operator	Precedence	Associativity
:-	1200	xfx
?-	1200	fx
-->	1200	xfx
;	1100	xfy
,	1000	xfy
not	900	fy
is	700	xfx
>=	700	xfx
=<	700	xfx
>	700	xfx
<	700	xfx
=..	700	xfx
\=	700	xfx
=	700	xfx
-	500	fx
+	500	fx
-	500	yfx
+	500	yfx
*	400	yfx
/	400	yfx
mod	300	xfx

INDEX